2-

WILLIAM WALLACE
The King's Enemy

Sprint

410- 60 60

WILLIAM WALLACE
The King's Enemy

D.J. GRAY

ROBERT HALE · LONDON

ISBN 0 7090 4329 5 (*paperback*)

Robert Hale Limited
Clerkenwell House
Clerkenwell Green
London EC1R 0HT

Photoset in North Wales by
Derek Doyle & Associates, Mold, Clwyd.
Printed in Great Britain by
St Edmundsbury Press, Bury St Edmunds, Suffolk.
Bound by WBC Bookbinders Limited.

Contents

The chronicler John of Fordun in his *Annals* wrote one of the most dramatic lines in Scottish history: 'In 1297, William Wallace lifted up his head.'

In that year the Scottish War of Independence broke out at the instigation of three men, of whom Wallace is the most famous.

His courage and determination to shake off the bonds of tyranny, and to resist oppression by a foreign power at all costs, remain an inspiration to this day.

SCOTLAND, *c.*1300

0   20   40   60 miles
0 20 40 60 80 100 km

Hebrides

Caithness

Sutherland

Ross

Skye

Cromarty

Moray Firth

Inverness

Buckie

Moray

River Spey

Banff

Badenoch

Aberdeen

Fort William

Athol

Brechin

Mull

Oban

Mentieth

Scone

Dundee

Lennox

Perth

St Andrews

Antonine
Wall

Stirling

River
Tay

River

Clyde

Falkirk

Dunfermline

Firth of Forth

Glasgow

Edinburgh

Dunbar

Irvine

Lothian

Cunningham

Berwick

Ayr

Kyle

River Tweed

Carrick

Lochmaben

Forest
of
Selkirk

Galloway

Dumfries

Caerlaverock

Annan

Kintyre

Solway Firth

Carlisle

1   *The Background*

Our old enemies come of Saxon's blood,
That never yet to Scotland would do
good.

Blind Harry

The history of the relationship between England and Scotland is a seesaw of power shifting first one way, then another. There were Scottish kings who initiated unwise invasions into the northern counties of England, in support of territorial aims or foreign usurpers, and thus lost their country's independence. And there were English rulers who were willing to sell that independence for money to underwrite their crusades in the Holy Land.

Scotland was certainly Romanized after Julius Caesar's invasion but to a far lesser extent than England. Geographically, Scotland was further removed from the centres of European culture than England. Large tracts, even in the Middle Ages, were uninhabited, except by wolves, eagles and wild boar.

Agricola in AD 80 built a line of forts between the Firths of Forth and Clyde and so marked a boundary between the ferocious Picts in the north and the more civilized south. Hadrian's Wall, erected in AD 120 between the Solway and the Tyne, was more an abandonment of a country which had proved of little benefit to Rome than an attempt to keep out the northern tribes.

The Romans had, in fact, come to accept that '... a victory in Scotland was never more than a prelude to defeat.'[1]

Although Severus in AD 208 broached the boundaries of Roman occupation and marched north, he lost 50,000 legionaries to the barbarians before succeeding in forcing terms on the Caledonians.

During the next hundred years, there were endless raids by the Picts from the north, the Scots from the western shores, and the Saxons from the east, into the territory south of the Tyne and Solway. But when Rome fell, in AD 410, its 300-year-old rule over Scotland ended, having had vastly less influence than in England, where roads had been built between towns and settlements, and the inhabitants had adopted the Roman way of life. Their presence north of Hadrian's Wall had amounted to little more than a military holding of territory which had never been subdued.

One hundred and fifty years after the end of Roman occupation in Scotland, the country was divided between four tribes: Scot, Pict, Briton and Angle, all fierce rivals and the forerunners of the Scottish nation.

Around the year 563 Columba brought Christianity from Ireland to Iona, and Scotland began to move out of her pagan darkness.

About AD 850 the Picts and Scots were united under Kenneth MacAlpin and gradually annexed their less powerful neighbours to become the kingdom of Alban.[2]

Between 1005 and 1034, Malcolm II of Alban made great efforts to unite the peoples he ruled and to extend his territories into those parts of England closest to the Borders. His first invasion of Lothian failed, and it was twelve years before he made another attempt at its annexation.

In 1018 a comet visible to the Northumbrians for thirty nights foretold a disaster which was not long in arriving. Their army was defeated at the Battle of Carham near Kelso by Malcolm's forces, and all their territory north of the River Tweed was ceded to Scotland.[3] The acquisition of Lothian meant, in effect, the transference of a separate English-speaking race to another country. This separateness was particularly noticeable in the thirteenth century, when Lothian stood apart and made no effort to support the struggle for independence from 1297 to 1304, nor from 1306 to 1314.[4] In 1310 it still held out, and Bruce was to invade it in an attempt to destroy once and for all its adherence to England.[5]

Thus it was Alban which created both medieval and modern Scotland, and its people never forgot that it was they who had conquered the south to unite the kingdom.[6]

One of Malcolm's daughters had been given in marriage to Sigmund the Stout, a Norwegian who held the northern mainland of Scotland. On Sigmund's death, his son Thorfinn conferred on Malcolm Caithness and Sutherland, thus leaving only the Western Isles, Orkney and Shetland, in Norwegian hands.

With these newly acquired territories, Scotland was now moving towards national unity, although certain areas, such as Moray and Galloway, were to be a source of trouble for years to come.

Although the Scots were nominally Christian, the old Celtic religion was held to by the majority of the people, while the Celtic traditions of loyalty to family and blood were as important in the northern Scotland of the thirteenth century as they had been in Malcolm's reign.[7]

Virtually nothing written exists from the eleventh century, apart from the Book of Deer, about conditions under Malcolm II.[8] England had the works of King Alfred, Bede and Caedmon, as well as manuscripts describing social and religious life which were compiled by its monastic houses. Scotland, instead, had a bardic tradition of word of mouth; of minstrels moving from one great hall to another with tales of past battles and invincible heroes. Stirring as they must have been, they are lost to us for ever, and even the life of such a man as William Wallace 300 years later contains gaps which can be filled only by folklore or those scraps of documentation which remain.

Malcolm III (r.1057–93) had spent his early life at the Court of Edward the Confessor. He had seen how England had become a united nation which, unless checked, was going to prove dangerous to Scotland's independence. Accordingly, he came to the Scottish throne determined to extend his borders south as far as the River Tees and thus strengthen his country. He invaded five times, forcing England to build or repair four of its principal strongholds in the north, Carlisle, Durham, Newcastle and Norham, in an effort to defend its northern territories.

The Norman Conquest in 1066 affected Scotland less immediately or profoundly than it did England, and when William the Conqueror invaded Scotland, Malcolm soon made peace with him. Many Norman knights acquired their vast estates in Scotland through intermarriage with Celtic heiresses, themselves descended from robber barons.[9] These Normans were already part-Celtic and readily fitted in with the Scottish Celts.

David I (r.1124–53) had spent much of his early life in England and came to the Scottish throne backed by Norman support. It had already helped secure him his earldom against his brother, Alexander, and his gratitude on his succession was expressed by gifts of land to favoured Norman nobles, such as de Brus and Fitz-Alan.[10]

His marriage to Matilda, granddaughter of Siward of Northumbria, brought him land in six English counties, the earldom of Northampton during her lifetime, and thereafter a claim to the earldom of Northumberland in his own right. The Scottish Border under his vigorous rule was extended to the Eden and the Tees, and the country became more firmly consolidated during his reign.

In 1127, as earl of Northampton, David was one of the English barons who took an oath acknowledging Henry I's daughter, Matilda, as his heir, and relations between the two countries were at the time peaceful and friendly.

However, during a second visit by David to the English Court in 1130, the rival House of Moray in the north of Scotland made an attempt to seize power. The province had always been a source of trouble, its rulers striving to seize the crown, and one of them, Macbeth, succeeding, to become one of the country's most able rulers.[11]

Moray differed from other earldoms by reason of a large number of men known as 'the freemen of Moray', who held their lands on condition that they gave the king military aid. They were, in effect, a company of king's men who owned no feudal superior other than the rightful monarch, and were responsible for the garrisoning of royal castles. Their lands were called 'castle lands' and were distinct from other Crown lands, whose owners merely raised their vassals in times of war but did not have the honour of garrisoning the king's fortifications.

The province had a banner of its own – *Vexillum Moraviae* – which all who were granted their lands from the king, whether nobles or thanes, were bound to follow.[12] Other feudal vassals followed the banner of whichever earl they served.

David, however, had left his kingdom in capable hands, and the Moray uprising was crushed at Stracathro in Fife.

Moray was to play an important part in the Scottish War of Independence, in which its unique position as a province owing allegiance directly to the monarch, and not to feudal superiors, placed it firmly on the side of Balliol. In 1290 the Earl of Mar was to describe it as a province under the immediate government of the king.[13]

After Henry I's death, David became involved in the struggle between Stephen, Count of Blois, who seized the English throne despite his oath of loyalty, and Empress Matilda. So bitter was the war that broke out between their respective forces that a popular saying declared that Christ and his saints were asleep.

David continued to support his niece, but only in so far as it did not interfere with Scottish affairs.

In 1136, with a view to seizing as much land as he could while English affairs were in a state of confusion, David launched an invasion, but after two weeks of stand-off negotiation at Newcastle, he agreed to a truce. As compensation, David's son, Henry, received the Honour of Huntingdon, an ancient earldom granted to Scottish Kings until 1237, and the castles of Carlisle and Doncaster. The peace was, however, short-lived. Soon the Scots were again on the offensive, this time meeting the English at Northallerton in Yorkshire at the Battle of the Standard. The Scots army consisted of Norman knights, German mercenaries, Norwegians from Orkney, Angles from Lothian and Alban Scots, but it failed to prevail against Stephen's better-disciplined forces and was heavily defeated.

David's plan for extending his Scottish territories thus received a severe check, but Stephen was obliged, after making peace in April 1139, to return to his struggle against Matilda without having managed to secure the restoration of his northern territories. For the remainder of David's reign, the River Eden in Cumberland and the River Tees between Durham and Yorkshire marked the boundary line between Scotland and England.

It was David who made the Church of Rome the national Church in Scotland, in addition founding all the great abbeys: Kelso, Dryburgh, Melrose, Cambuskenneth, Holyrood and Jedburgh.

During his reign, the Comyns, who claimed descent from Donald Bane, the eleventh-century Scottish king, and who were to play a vital part in the War of Independence, came into being.[14] The nephew of David's chancellor, William Cumin, married the daughter of an influential Northumberland family and became the first Comyn.[15] One branch of the family became earls of Buchan through marriage.[16] Another was granted Badenoch in 1229 by Alexander II and spread to Lochaber, holding Urquhart and Inverlochy Castles as Wardens of the Great Glen.[17] By the thirteenth century, the family included four earls – Buchan, Menteith, Angus and Atholl – and thirty-two knights.

In 1297, between them, the Earl of Buchan and John Comyn 'the Red' controlled the entire district from Buchan to Lochaber, and from 1301 until 1304 organized resistance to English domination was due almost wholly to the Comyns. It was in the Celtic north that the real hostility lay against England.[18]

David I's heir having died, he was succeeded in 1153 by his grandson, Malcolm IV, a frail child aged twelve.[19] Now it was Scotland's turn to suffer internal strife, as rival factions strove to gain the ascendancy, while in England Henry II (r.1154–89) had a firm grip on his country's affairs.

In 1157 he met Malcolm at Chester and laid down his conditions for continuing friendly relations with Scotland.

These included the return of the counties of Durham, Northumberland and Westmorland, which David had annexed. The young Malcolm was dependent on his advisers, Norman knights who owned territories in both countries. Considering Henry II the better prospect for their future, they urged Malcolm to accept. It would have been unrealistic to expect a boy of sixteen to do other than propitiate such a powerful neighbouring monarch, and the seesaw of power swung now in England's favour.

Leaving Scotland to those nobles better equipped to direct its destiny than himself, Malcolm took part in Henry's war against France and fought at Toulouse in 1159. In 1163 he again met the English king, this time at Woodstock, where he did homage to his son, Henry, heir to the throne. In 1165 Malcolm died and was succeeded by his brother, William the Lyon, who was to rule Scotland for forty-nine years.

At first, the signs for Scotland's future were encouraging, but in 1174 William made a disastrous decision that was to have far-reaching effects on his country, when he agreed to support Prince Henry in a conspiracy against his father.[20] A Scots army invaded Northumberland and ravaged the countryside with extreme brutality. Unable to proceed further, the Scots turned west, captured several castles and besieged Carlisle.

In July of the same year, William was seized by a well-armed force consisting of barons from Yorkshire, and imprisoned by King Henry in the castle of Falaise. On 23 December 1174 he was forced to sign a treaty by which he became, in effect, a vassal of the English monarch. The castles of Berwick, Jedburgh, Edinburgh and Stirling were thenceforth to be garrisoned by English troops, and William's brother David with twenty-one Scottish knights was surrendered as a hostage as evidence of his good faith.

The result in Scotland was an upsurge of resentment among its people at this English interference in the country's affairs, Galloway, with its hatred of all things Norman, being especially unruly. While England continued to make progress towards national unity, and her trade with the Continent benefited in consequence, Scotland's development was continuously disrupted by internal squabbles due to a lack of confidence in its king.

In 1189, however, Henry II died and was succeeded by Richard I. The Lionheart's ambition was to mount a third crusade to capture Jerusalem, an undertaking which required large sums of money, while during his absence it was essential to have a friendly monarch as his immediate neighbour.[21] For William's gift of 10,000 marks, Richard restored Scotland's independence and handed back Berwick and Roxburgh Castles.

When John succeeded in 1199, he endeavoured to build a larger fortress at Berwick to protect his northern counties, but his efforts were continually hindered by Scottish raids. In 1209 he invaded Scotland with so intimidating an army that William bought him off with a payment of 15,000 marks.

Although William's endless conciliation of England during his reign was a source of irritation to his people, it did ensure peace – or, at least, no serious conflict – between the two countries, which lasted for more than a century.

Alexander II came to the throne in 1214, with England now in turmoil under John. Twice Alexander led an army into England, in support of those English barons who offered to make him master of the three northern counties if he would back them.

In 1216 Henry III, a boy of nine, succeeded to the throne, and at once the English barons deserted Alexander. Determined to retain his hold on the northern counties, Alexander enlisted the help of Louis, the eldest son of Philip Augustus, King of France, but the invading French army was defeated at Lincoln. In 1217, at Berwick, Alexander was obliged to accept a treaty that involved his abandoning all claim to the disputed counties.

In 1221 Alexander married Henry's sister Joanna, while his own sister Margaret became the wife of Hubert de Burgh, the most powerful baron in England and, therefore, a useful ally.

Henry III, however, was not content to let peaceful

conditions continue between himself and Alexander, and decided to assert those claims which William the Lyon had yielded at Falaise. He induced the Pope, Gregory IX, to put pressure on Alexander, who promptly renewed his own claim to the northern counties and set about preparing for war.

In September 1237, at York, the long-standing dispute was finally laid to rest.[22] Alexander abandoned his claims but retained the Honour of Huntingdon and the lands and dwellings of ten English counties, together with grants of land in Cumberland and Northumberland, to the annual value of £200.

In 1249 Alexander II died at Kerrera in the Bay of Oban while on a journey to the Western Isles.[23]

Alexander III's reign, from 1249 to 1286, is known as 'Scotland's golden age'.[24] It began, however, with the customary upsets and internal rivalries, which were to last for nine years. The divided loyalties of barons who held land under both Alexander and Henry III was to evolve into two parties. The first of these consisted of nobles who were Norman by birth and tradition. They could see advantages to themselves if Alexander were made a vassal of England, for it would ensure the continuing security of their possessions in both countries. Opposing them were those Normans mixed with Celts, mostly from north of the River Forth, who would eventually become the national party which was to fight for their country's independence in the thirteenth century. It was led by one of the most powerful barons in Scotland, Walter Comyn, Earl of Menteith, the ancestor of Wallace's betrayer.

Comyn's opponent was Alan Durward, the High Justiciary, married to a natural daughter of the late Alexander II, an ambitious man determined to seize power while the King remained a minor.

Meanwhile, Henry III was not averse to causing what trouble he could for his neighbour north of the Borders. Having appealed to the Pope to declare Alexander his feudal inferior and been turned down, Henry soon found himself too deeply involved in internal problems to take advantage of the situation in Scotland.

When at York, in 1251, for the marriage of his daughter Margaret, aged ten, to 11-year-old Alexander, Henry made a gesture of good-will by warning that Alan Durward was plotting to seize power.[25] Durward fled to France, but in 1254 he resurfaced in Scotland. With his supporters, the Earls of March, Strathearn and Carrick, Robert de Brus and Alexander, Steward of Scotland, he seized the young couple and carried them off to Kelso Abbey. Henry III then invaded with an army before the regency could muster its defence, and at the resultant meeting at the abbey terms were agreed that made the English King virtual master of Scotland. Twenty-one new regents were named, chief among them being Alan Durward.

The Comyns, however, continued to plot, and in 1257 they in turn seized Alexander and Margaret at Kinross and placed them for safekeeping in Stirling Castle.[26] Durward fled with the remnants of his regency, while the Comyns set about gathering an army at Jedburgh. This time it was a resentful Henry who was obliged to give way, and in 1259 the Earls of Hereford and Albemarle and the Scots-Norman John de Balliol arrived at Melrose to make peace. Ten new regents were appointed, six of them coming from Comyn's national party, and a semblance of peace returned to Scotland.

In 1261, when he was twenty-one, Alexander paid a state visit to London and was fêted in the capital. His relations with both Henry III and Edward I remained cordial until his death in 1286.[27]

In 1266 Norway ceded the Western Isles and the Isle of Man to Scotland for a sum of 4,000 marks and an annual fee of 100 marks.[28] Now only Orkney and Shetland remained in Norwegian hands.

And in 1278 Alexander took an oath of allegiance at a parliament at Westminster as 'liegeman of the lord Edward, king of the English', who had ascended the throne in 1272, bending his knee to the man who was to devote the energies of a lifetime to the total subjugation of Alexander's countrymen.[29]

2 Scotland

This little land of Scotia beyond which there is no human
habitation.
Letter to Pope John XXII in 1320 by the barons of Scotland.

Scotland in the thirteenth century was a prosperous,
evolving country, whose military tradition had been
allowed to lapse after years of peace with England. Its
population was probably not many more than 400,000 in
1300.[1]

There was a north–south divide occasioned by the
Antonine Line, an imaginary line drawn from north of
Renfrew on the Firth of Clyde to Bo'ness on the Firth of
Forth.[2] North of it, the country was almost wholly Celtic.
By temperament and character the Scots had the
reputation of being 'a warlike and independent race',
quick to take to armed resistance in defence of their
freedom.[3] A later writer was to say: 'They [the
Highlanders] were the best natural material for soldiers on
earth ... That made them a peril to the State.'[4]

It was in the old Celtic kingdom north of the Forth and
Clyde that unyielding hostility to England lay.[5] All the
chief participants of the War of Independence of 1297
were Celts: William Wallace, Andrew de Moray and
David, the Bishop of Moray and Caithness, while Robert
Bruce claimed Celtic heritage through his mother.

Political and religious refugees had settled in the
country and formed influential centres of trade and
culture. Aberdeen and Berwick both had large Flemish
communities.[6] There were exports of wool, hides, furs
such as pine marten and coney, timber and fish to
England, the Low Countries, Scandinavia and the
Hanseatic League, as well as luxury goods, such as pearls

from the River Tay, amethysts and semi-precious stones from the Cairngorms, and fine silver brooches.[7] Fattened beef animals were driven from the Western Highlands along drovers' roads into England to fetch the best prices, while the currencies of both countries were inter-changeable.[8]

The most valuable parts of the country were in the hands of families of Norman and Saxon descent.[9] Much of it, however, remained wild and untamed, particularly in the Highlands, where agriculture was difficult and confined to smallholdings.[10] Most settlements and towns were close to the coast, so that the land could be farmed and the trade of fishing carried on, or sprang up at places where rivers could be forded or bridged.[11]

Few journeys were made by sea, apart from merchant vessels which were at the mercy of privateers.[12] It took eighteen days to travel by horse from Berwick to London, which included a stopover of four days at York.[13] For a dispatch to be carried to London and an answer returned took the best part of a month.

There were no roads as such, and many tracks were impassable in winter or heavy rain.[14] Forests stretched for immense distances, interspersed with moors, boglands or ravines, and were the haunt of all manner of wild game. Selkirk Forest, in which Wallace was often to take refuge, stretched apparently from the Borders to north of the River Forth.[15] To these forests were attracted outlaws, fugitives from justice, and 'broken men' – that is, those who had been dispossessed of their land through dispute with their feudal lord.

The feudal system had been brought to Scotland by the Norman barons who arrived in the train of William the Conqueror. On being granted land by his ruler, a noble would set about building a castle, to which were attached market centres (burghs).[16] He would then lease out those parts of his estate not required by himself to vassals, who promised him loyalty, and aid in time of war. In return, they would divide their portion into smaller estates and lease them out to minor knights.[17] A vassal, then, might find himself fighting on the side of his overlord, or overlord's overlord, whether or not he supported his cause. Failure to do so meant being turned off his land and losing his livelihood.

Those barons who held land in both countries came to suffer divided loyalties. Their fear of losing their more productive English possessions accounted for many Scottish nobles' changing sides during the War of Independence. By upbringing and descent they were Norman, and their involvement with Scotland amounted in many cases to little more than land and lordship. Edward I was adept at rewarding those Scottish knights who adhered to him with gifts of land and remittance of their debts, and in this way kept hold on their loyalty.

In the twelfth century, there were a considerable number of free burghs, which had the monopoly of trade within a certain area and paid no taxes on the transfer of their goods. They were free to elect their own magistrates, but only those who owned property in the burgh could enjoy its privileges. If a man purchased a holding and occupied it unclaimed for a year and a day, a knight's or baron's thrall became a freeman and a privileged burgess of the town.

Twelve burgesses, chosen by the mayor or aldermen, were required, under threat of a fine, to attend courts (eyres) held by the lord chamberlain acting as the king's representative. Their object was to ensure that money due to the monarch was forthcoming and that tradesmen in the community were acting honestly.

Bakers and butchers had to place their foodstuffs for sale in full view. Failure to do so meant confiscation and their goods given to the needy. Certain trades were regarded as more socially acceptable than others. No magistrate might bake bread or brew ale except for his personal use. Butchers, dyers and shoemakers had to renounce their trades before becoming burgesses. The most lucrative trade was in cloth. Only burgesses were allowed to buy or sell it, or purchase and dye wool. Fish was an important item for medieval Christians, especially during Lent, and it required salt for curing, so salt became an important trading commodity.[18] 'Unsocial' crafts, such as those of tanners and butchers, were allocated specific areas in their town, where they could prove less offensive.[19]

Every fortnight a court was held which dealt with those who had broken the law, and three times a year, at Easter, Michaelmas and Christmas, a moot assembled to consider matters relating directly to the burgh itself. There was an annual fair, when those who had offended at law could be granted immunity, except those accused of serious crimes. There was also a weekly market held on a fixed day.[20]

Every town had a hospital for lepers, whose movements were strictly controlled, while the infirmarian at the nearest monastery would treat the general sick with potions made from his herb garden.[21] In villages there would be a 'wise woman', able to help mothers in childbirth and dispense remedies for run-of-the-mill ailments. Medical knowledge was, however, slight, and more men died from infected wounds than were actually killed in conflict.[22] Infant mortality was high in the Middle Ages.[23] Holy wells were held in great esteem, and any number of superstitious beliefs which had come down from pagan times, such as the ancient fire festival on 31 October and bowing to the new moon, still held sway.

In all towns of any importance was a castle, in which the governor, as representative of the monarch, protected the king's interests and defended the area against attack. Every able-bodied man took his turn at keeping watch from curfew to daybreak.

Education was considered important only for the well-to-do and was in the hands of the Church, the one institution in the Middle Ages which could be described as touching the lives of every citizen.

When Edward determined to anglicize the Scottish Church in 1296, it was an act that raised widespread indignation. The Catholic Church in Scotland was always relentlessly opposed to the domination of England.[24] Interference by an outside agency was interpreted as an attempt to undermine Scottish life at its very roots. The Church was the centre of town and village life, and to find Scottish incumbents replaced by English clerics aroused the deepest resentment in all classes.

It is said that, during Wallace's activities in May and

June 1297, many of these English priests and nuns were driven out of their dioceses and in some cases killed if they resisted, such was the depth of Scottish hatred for the interlopers.[25]

After the Church in importance was the army. A standing army, as such, did not exist, for the cost of keeping a large number of men for long periods of idleness between wars would have been an enormous drain on the state's finances. When soldiers were needed, the monarch's nobles provided men, arms and horses under their terms of feudal fealty, and so on down the line.

Foreign service was unpopular. Edward I, in particular, endeavoured to enlist large numbers of soldiers, paid and unpaid, for his wars in Europe, an action which was to cause a crisis in England in 1297.[26] Such was the opposition of his barons that he was obliged to sail for Flanders with only a hundred knights and 570 squires.[27]

The Scottish tradition on fighting was on foot, principally because so much of the country was unsuited to horses.[28] Wallace had comparatively few mounted soldiers. In any battle, the main fighting was done by the heavy cavalry. Its knights were professionals who had the financial backing of huge estates granted them by the king, and kept their skills at a high level of excellence by engaging in feats of arms at tourneys. A knight taking part in tournaments had the chance of winning worthwhile prizes. If his opponent was captured, he would receive a ransom to free him, and if a horse was captured, it became the victor's property.[29]

Horses were bred specially to bear the weight of an armed rider, and the loss of one placed a serious financial burden on its owner.[30] When Sir William Douglas changed sides so precipitously in 1301, he made off with a friend's horse which the king himself replaced.

There were two classes of horse soldiers, light cavalry and heavy.[31] The latter consisted of horses fully protected by armour, with mailed riders. Light cavalry meant unprotected horses, which were highly vulnerable to the twelve-foot spears with which the Scots infantry was armed. At Falkirk, the Scottish schiltrons were surrounded by banks of dead and dying horses impaled on their pikes. The schiltron, which was possibly devised by Wallace himself, was a hedgehog formation of soldiers kneeling in front, with their spears sloping outwards, the ranks behind, similarly armed, successively rising. Once on foot, a heavily armoured knight was unable to move quickly, and considerable physical stamina was required to lay about him with his sword in the fierce mêlée of a battle.

In addition to his horse, a knight would have individually made armour from a skilled craftsman, while his shield, sword, battle-axe and lance involved a considerable outlay. A mounted knight wore a padded garment underneath his armour called a gambeson, with chainmail hose and gloves, and a conical iron helmet.[32] Under its trappings of silk, his destrier was as well armoured as its master. He would also have squires, grooms and body-servants to attend to himself and his horse.

There were also archers in any army, few in the Scottish force apart from some Borderers, but more among the English, chiefly mercenaries from South Wales.[33] Bowmen, in fact, formed an important part of the English army, and the longbow, used for the first time to any extent in the Battle of Falkirk, 1298, was to usher in the superiority of English archers who were to wreak such havoc at Crécy and Agincourt.

The crossbow, which was disliked by the chivalrous as a particularly murderous weapon, had been banned by the Lateran Council in 1139.[34] This merely emphasized its formidable killing-power, and it was adopted enthusiastically by those Gascon mercenaries who formed part of Edward's army.

Every freeman was expected to fight when required to do so, but many had virtually no military training and may have done little more than make up the numbers.[35]

In time of war, the sheriffs of certain counties would be ordered to raise so many men, who would be armed partly at their own expense and partly as a charge to the county.[36] Unskilled labourers received wages from the day of their joining, but if they were called upon to defend their home county, they were not paid.

They wore an acton, which was a padded leather jacket, and a basnet, a steel head-covering, and would carry whatever weapons they had: knives, swords or home-made pikes. Those who could not provide an acton would wear a habergeon, a chain neck-covering, and an iron jack, which consisted of back and breast pieces, and a conical steel helmet.[37]

They were not, of course, called upon to make any decision as to which side they fought on. Ordinary citizens had no voice in the government of their country. They were not consulted over the matter of the royal succession.

One man was to change all that and to give the common people a decisive opportunity to declare their courageous determination to be free of a foreign yoke.

That man was William Wallace.

3 *William Wallace*

Of whole lineage and true line of Scotland.
Blind Harry

If there were monks in the south of Scotland, illuminating manuscripts and keeping records of life in the thirteenth century, their monasteries were so often destroyed during Edward I's repeated invasions that not a line survives. Many official documents were removed to England in 1296 and were never seen again.[1]

There are, therefore, gaps in the life of Scotland's great patriot, William Wallace, but it should never be imagined that, because his name cannot be found in historical annals, he was either inactive or had given up the fight. His character utterly refutes that, for he was young, enthusiastic and, above all, passionate. That one word, indeed, more than any other describes all of Wallace's actions.

He was imbued with a love of freedom that time and again put his life at risk. He could not accept that his country had been occupied by foreign troops, nor its citizens placed under the jurisdiction of any monarch other than the rightfully crowned king of Scotland. He burned with a young man's desire to free Scotland, and it is noticeable that his closest friends and supporters all shared his youth. His enthusiasm was to kindle a responding chord in the hearts of the Scottish people, so that they rose like a tide to join him.

The one man who feared that his influence would forever deny him the conquest of Scotland was Edward I. Even when every Scottish noble of standing had yielded to the English king, and Scotland lay exhausted from endless invasions, it was Wallace whom Edward pursued relentlessly to a death that aroused in his countrymen an undying hatred of all things English.

More than one date is given for Wallace's birth, but it is generally accepted as 1274, the same year in which Robert Bruce, the future king, was born.[2]

Blind Harry, the poet, muddled his dates and put Wallace as forty-five at the time of his death in 1305. However, in 1297, at the Battle of Stirling Bridge, Wallace was described by the chroniclers as '*juvenis*', 'a young man'.[3] If 1274 is taken as being reasonably accurate, Wallace was twenty-three or twenty-four at Stirling Bridge. Harry also gives December 1296 for the Selby incident at Dundee: this would make Wallace nineteen at Stirling Bridge, admittedly not impossible, but one must treat Harry's dates with caution.[4] A further pointer to his youth is that in 1296 his maternal grandfather held the position of Sheriff of Ayr, and he was still alive in 1307 as an active supporter of Bruce.[5]

William was the second son of Sir Malcolm Wallace of Elderslie in the county of Renfrew. He held his land under James the Steward, whose father had been one of Alexander III's chief councillors. The family motto was '*Esperance*' – 'Hope'.[6]

The family could trace its lineage to the influential Fitz-Alans. In 1174 Richard Wallensis, a vassal of Walter Fitz-Alan, was appointed Steward of Scotland by David I, and was one of the witnesses of the foundation of Paisley monastery.[7] The name Wallensis or Le Waleys may have been originally Welsh, and indicate that the family came from the Welsh Marches to Scotland with Walter Fitz-Alan. There are at least twenty-one different spellings of the name.[8]

The family was an extensive one, incorporating the Wallaces of Riccarton and Elderslie and others scattered through Renfrew. It had certainly been settled in Scotland for over a century.[9] Harry's description is frequently quoted: Wallace was 'of whole lineage and true line of Scotland'.[10]

Wallace's mother was Margaret de Crauford, daughter of Sir Reginald de Crauford of Loudon, the Sheriff of

Ayr.[11] Her family was of Danish origin and came from Northumberland. Thorlongus, an Anglo-Danish chief, had been granted lands in the Merse by King Edgar at the beginning of the twelfth century.[12] When displaced by William the Conqueror, Wallace's great-grandfather married the heiress of Loudon and was created first hereditary Sheriff of Ayr.

Wallace's elder brother was also named Malcolm, and there was a younger brother, John, who was one of William's first allies. There may have been two older sisters, both married.[13]

Wallace would have grown up in what would now be comparable to the home of a well-to-do country gentleman, whose feudal vassals paid rent by making their services available when required.[14] He would learn his first letters quite possibly from his mother, and indulge in such pursuits as horsemanship, hunting and mock battles with his brothers.

His love of freedom must first have been aroused by Sir Malcolm, for this courageous knight refused to make obeisance to Edward and is believed in consequence to have been killed by an English officer named Fenwick in 1296.[15]

Another important influence on Wallace's boyhood was that of an uncle, a brother of his father, who was a cleric at Dunipace, a chapelry of Cambuskenneth Abbey. Harry describes him as being wealthy and 'a full kind man'.[16] He is credited with teaching Wallace not only Latin but words which became the boy's favourite saying: *'Dico tibi verum, libertas optima rerum: nunquam servili sub nexu vivito, fili'* – 'Freedom is best, I tell thee true, of all things to be won. Then never live within the bond of slavery, my son.'[17] Another uncle, also a priest, resided at Kilspindie, ten miles from Dundee, and was also to play a part in Wallace's career.

By the time Wallace was sent to be schooled at Paisley Abbey, he must already have shown signs of the strong, vigorous and commanding figure he was to become, at a time when contemporary suits of armour show their wearers to have been on average five feet five inches. Edward I's height of over six feet is frequently referred to by his chroniclers as worthy of mention, and it is impossible to imagine Wallace's inspiring his countrymen to deeds of valour had he been a small, short figure of retiring disposition. He is said to have had brown wavy hair and to have been 'of goodly mien'.[18]

He could read and write in three languages, his own, Latin and French. He spoke Gaelic, and had studied ancient and modern history and the science of his day.[19]

When older, Wallace was sent for further education to Dundee, where he met a number of like-minded spirits, and lodged with his uncle at Kilspindie.[20] If this move occurred in 1291, when he was about seventeen years of age, it was at a time when Edward had begun to tighten his grip on Scotland. His forces had seized the Isle of Man during the previous year, and in 1291 he had ordered every Scottish castle placed under English control. On his progress to Perth, all classes had been forced to pay him homage, those refusing to do so being at once arrested.

Kilspindie is ten miles from Dundee, which in turn is five from Perth. It is tempting to wonder if, among the silent crowds watching Edward ride by, attended by his retinue of knights, all representing English domination in a country that was not his, was the young William Wallace. If so, perhaps it was at that moment that his passionate intention to drive these arrogant usurpers out of Scotland sprang into being.

Among Wallace's friends at this time were Duncan of Lorn, Sir Niel Campbell of Lochawe and John Blair, who subsequently entered the Order of Benedictines but left the cloister to become Wallace's personal chaplain. When in retirement, possibly at Dunfermline Abbey, he wrote the biography of Wallace which was to form the basis for Harry's eulogy.[21]

Harry's work, entitled *The Life and Acts of Sir William Wallace of Ellerslie by Henry the Minstrel*, was written during the reign of James IV (1488–1513). It has frequently come in for a good deal of denigration for its inaccuracies as to dates and his poetic licence in crediting Wallace with other men's exploits, as well as impossible deeds of valour, but it is constructed on solid fact. Nor must it be forgotten that Harry drew on the Latin writings of John Blair, and while the Benedictine may have seen his departed friend through the rose-hued light of an intense loyalty, he had known Wallace since Dundee and had no need to invent episodes when the truth was well known to any number of people still alive.[22] In addition, the poet had the patronage of his hero's namesake and descendant, Sir William Wallace of Craigie, who undoubtedly passed on to him family traditions and tales which had never been written down.[23]

Although Harry is said to have been born blind,[24] he himself reported that he had read Blair's writings in his youth, and another *Life* by Sir Thomas Gray, parson of Liberton. It is likely the minstrel became blind in later life, but this might only have sharpened his recollection.

His poem contains 11,861 lines in rhyming couplets and exists in a manuscript dated 1488.[25] The first to mention Harry was John Major, whose *De Gestis Scotorum* was published in 1521. He calls him 'Henry' and avers he had written a book about Wallace, 'weaving the common stories ... into a vernacular poetry, in which he was skilled'. Wallace's integrity shines through in every line.[26] The poem has certainly enshrined Wallace in every patriotic Scotsman's heart, thus preserving the love and devotion with which he was regarded by his countrymen during and long after his lifetime.

While Wallace was at Dundee, landowners and men of substance were ordered to appear before the newly appointed English deputies to give their oath of allegiance to England. Sir Malcolm Wallace made no attempt to appear at Ayr, nor to send any excuse for not doing so, and from that moment he was a marked man. Wisely, he slipped away to Lennox with his eldest son until he considered it safe to return. Possibly at Loudon Hill, overlooking the Firth of Clyde on the River Irvine, he was overtaken and killed by a party of English soldiers.[27]

The news must have come as a devastating blow to Wallace. Sir Reginald Crauford, his uncle, considering it unwise to resist at this time, had submitted and been confirmed as the continuing Sheriff of Ayr, and other members of the family had followed his example. Only Sir

Malcolm had held out, and Sir Reginald, anxious for Lady Wallace's safety, sent her to Kilspindie, in the Carse of Gowrie.[28]

That the injustice of his father's death burned deeply into the 17-year-old's heart is evidenced by what might be called 'the Selby incident'. This occurred in either December 1291 or January 1292. It represented Wallace's first serious brush with the English authorities and was to set his foot on a path leading to the historic Battle of Stirling Bridge, six years later.

Nothing is more deeply resented by a free people than the presence of an occupying force. It is not difficult to imagine the English garrison from Dundee Castle mocking the citizenry for their incomprehensible broad Scots or Gaelic, helping themselves openly from some merchant's stall or jostling aside those who impeded their way.

Wallace and his friends must have watched, in particular, the swaggering son of the English 'captain'.[29] His father was either deputy to the castle's governor, Sir Brian Fitz-Alan, or possibly the captain of Dundee itself. At any rate, young Selby and his cronies came upon Wallace, a young man whose height and impressive physical appearance must have drawn the eye.

Encounters of this nature, between young men on opposing sides, have occurred down the ages and broken off without either coming to serious harm. But in this case Selby made a fatal move. It is probable he already knew Wallace by sight. He may have heard of Sir Malcolm's death for failing to submit to Edward's authority and uttered an unwise, possibly taunting remark. Wallace, still grieving over his father's death, made an effort at control. But when Selby put his hand on the knife at Wallace's belt, perhaps sneering at him for cowardice, they were the last words he spoke. Wallace seized him by the collar and struck him a tremendous blow with his clenched fist that killed him.[30]

Beating off Selby's friends, Wallace fled through the streets of Dundee, making for a dwelling in which he and his uncle had often been entertained. With remarkably quick thinking, the lady of the house disguised him in one of her dresses, pulled a bonnet over his head and set him down with a distaff to spin.[31]

When the pursuers, joined by other English soldiers, thundered on the door to be admitted, there was no dishevelled assassin to be found. As they charged excitedly through the various rooms, they must scarcely have glanced at the servant girl busy in a corner of the kitchen. If there is one pointer that in 1291 Wallace was a beardless youth and not a 30-year-old man, it is the fact that he was able to pass on this occasion with cursory scrutiny as a young woman.

One may guess at the uproar that now seized Dundee as young Selby's attacker was sought, while the gates of the town were manned by extra guards to prevent Wallace's escape. The idea that he might be disguised in female attire had never occurred to the authorities.

It is not known how Wallace got out of Dundee.[32] Either he left openly on a wagon, huddled in shawls beside a male companion who pretended that the figure at his side was his wife, or he was smuggled on board a fishing-boat at night and landed some miles further up the River Tay. Once out of town, he made rapidly for the priest of Kilspindie.

Wallace's mother, on hearing the news, must have been distraught. If the authorities laid hands on her son, he would certainly hang.

His uncle, however, was as resourceful as the rest of the family, and it was in the guise of pilgrims travelling to the shrine of St Margaret at Dunfermline that, probably within a matter of hours, Wallace and his mother set off. At Dunipace they refused an invitation from their priestly kinsman to take refuge with him, and carried on to Elderslie and the family home.[33]

There Sir Reginald decided that his nephew, now declared an outlaw, would be safer with relations at Riccarton, near Kilmarnock, where there were fewer English to arouse his passions. Wallace was sent to them, with orders to keep him out of mischief.

Some years later, when Wallace was fighting in the west of Scotland, he received news of his mother's death. She had been forced to leave Elderslie once more, doubtless due to his activities, and died at Dunfermline. Unable to attend her burial, Wallace sent John Blair, the Benedictine, in his place.[34]

Between 1291 and 1296 there is little written evidence of Wallace's activities, apart from Harry's poem, but it would be unrealistic to believe that such a vigorous young man was content to remain docile and inactive with his relations. No doubt for some months he kept a low profile at Riccarton, but before long his friends from Dundee must have got in touch with him. Harry states that many of Wallace's most able supporters were members of his own family, and one can imagine young male cousins – and certainly female ones – visiting their dashing kinsman who had actually taken the life of one of the hated English.[35] The tales and discussions would continue well into the night, as Wallace passionately re-averred his resistance to the English occupation of his country.

Among those early allies of his were Sir Richard Wallace of Riccarton, head of the family, who gave him shelter at this time. His three sons all joined Wallace, the eldest, Adam, particularly distinguishing himself with his bravery. Wallace of Auchincruive, a cousin, and Edward Little and Tom Halliday, nephews, were also of this number. Halliday's eldest daughter was married to young Sir John the Graham, who was to become Wallace's second-in-command, while his second daughter was the wife of Johnstone, 'a man of good degree', who was ultimately appointed by Wallace governor of Lochmaben Castle. Other kinsmen were young Patrick Auchinleck of Gilbank, an uncle by marriage, Kilpatrick, related to Lady Wallace, and Kneland (or Cleland) and William Crauford, cousins.[36]

By now Wallace had broadened into a physically powerful young man, with brown, slightly curling hair and handsome features, and was possessed of that gift which defies description but which would now be called charisma. Men who offered their lives to Wallace's cause remained true to him despite all vicissitudes. At the Battle of Stirling Bridge, 10,000 troops under his command would remain in absolute obedience to his order to stand firm, as they watched the awesome English army's remorseless advance. In all his wanderings after the defeat at Falkirk, he was accompanied by a loyal band of friends, sometimes no more than four or five, but all as fiercely committed to freedom as himself.

4 Edward I

Scotorum malleus *(Hammer of the Scots)*
Epitaph on the tomb of Edward I

It is not only generals who need that added element of luck if they are to win battles against overwhelming odds. In the Middle Ages kings who were most successful at ruling their countries needed it, too. Edward I of England (r.1272–1307) survived accidents that would have killed lesser men. Alexander III of Scotland's good fortune deserted him at a time when his heir was a frail, 3-year-old girl child, and plunged Scotland into the bitter conflict of the War of Independence. Alexander was to be the last Celtic king of Scotland, and the last to be crowned on the hallowed Stone of Destiny at Scone.

It might be said that, had Edward been a lesser horseman and Alexander a better rider, William Wallace would have survived to share the honours of the Battle of Bannockburn in 1314, instead of being hacked to death in 1305 in the name of justice.

During one of his inspections of the sea defences at Winchelsea, Edward came as close to death as was possible, and survive.[1] The newly laid-out town, built following the gradual destruction of the orginal by storm and erosion, was surrounded on the side facing the harbour by a low earth wall. Between its battlements, one could look straight down onto the roadway below that wound its way up the cliffs.

While the King was riding along this embankment and admiring his fleet, now in a state of readiness for his invasion of Flanders, Edward's horse took fright. A nearby windmill's sails had started up suddenly and the animal, urged on by spurs and whip, plunged forward, terrified, over the wall. Those accompanying the King were certain he must have been thrown and killed. Instead, thanks to Edward's superb horsemanship, his mount landed squarely on the road, slid wildly for some way but remained upright. Not even attempting to dismount, Edward turned its head and rode calmly up to the town gates.

It is tempting to make this incident one of the 'ifs' of history. Had Edward's horse lost its footing, his son, the Prince of Wales, who was to become a weak, pleasure-loving young man addicted to male favourites, would have come to the throne ten years earlier than he did. The Battle of Stirling Bridge, which was to take place two months later, in September 1297, would not merely have been the decisive win it was for Wallace but have assured him of a long and distinguished career as adviser and general to King John Balliol.

Undoubtedly Edward put down his miraculous escape at Winchelsea to the special protection he received from his favourite saints. He favoured particularly the great shrine of the Blessed Virgin at Walsingham in Norfolk, whom he believed responsible for saving him once, while he was playing chess.[2] Suddenly he had felt impelled to move from the table, seconds before a stone block crashed from the roof onto the chair he had just occupied. He had also survived an assassin's attack while crusading in the Holy Land, and in Paris a lightning bolt missed him by a fraction, killing two attendants at his back.[3]

Edward I had a reputation for sanctity. The tomb of St Edward in Westminster Abbey was presented with the gold sceptre and crown and the silver orb which had been part of the Scottish regalia.[4] He travelled with a portable chapel mounted on a wagon drawn by two oxen, and two other holy relics he had plundered, the Black Rood of Scotland and the Cross Gneyth from Wales, received favoured attention.[5] In Glasgow, during August and September 1301, he made offerings at the shrine of St Kentigern, the amount being invariably 7 shillings, and to the friars of other religious orders.[6] When on a visit to Walsingham on 2 February 1298, he made a gift to the

Virgin of a gold brooch set with a cameo, which had also been removed from Edinburgh.[7]

Yet it is difficult to find a less attractive king than Edward I. There have been other English monarchs as ruthlessly determined to get their own way, ridding themselves of inconvenient advisers, children or wives, by turn crafty, underhand or downright wicked. For all of them one has a reluctant admiration absent in the case of Edward.

A contemporary admirer, Nicholas Trivet, described him as 'intolerant of injuries, and reckless of dangers when seeking revenge'.[8] He could forgive powerful barons such as Bruce and Comyn, however often they broke their oaths of allegiance to him, well aware that he depended on their support to control Scotland. Yet, towards a man who had never bent the knee to him, knowing he had nothing to gain by generosity or mercy, Edward was to order a death of barbaric cruelty. He could not bear opposition to his wishes, and at times indulged in bursts of frustrated rage which made him behave unjustly.[9]

He had, as men said – beneath their breath, if they were wise – the luck of the Devil; no empty phrase, for the Plantagenets derived from the sinister and greatly feared Angevins, whose reputation was one of 'unadulterated evil'.[10] Their legendary founding father was a Breton brigand called Tortulf the Forester. His descendant, Fulk the Red, attached himself to the dukes of France and was rewarded by being made first count of Anjou.

The name Plantagenet came from the sprig of *planta genista*, yellow broom, worn on the helmet in battle by Geoffrey the Handsome, Count of Anjou, the Angevin whose son became Henry II of England.[11] In her book *The God of the Witches*, Dr Margaret Murray suggests that the Plantagenets were linked through their Angevin ties to the very roots of European witchcraft. Long after Europe became Christian, the Germans remained unconverted, and the Angevin dynasty was said to have originated from a long line of pagans.[12]

Under William the Conqueror, Anjou lost its importance, but it revived early in the twelfth century with Fulk of Jerusalem. In order to secure the friendship of this powerful enemy, Henry suggested a marriage between his widowed daughter, Matilda, and Fulk's son, Geoffrey, that was to bring civil war to England.[13] Their son, who became Henry II, was the first Plantagenet. He added Aquitaine and Gascony to his possessions in France and is perhaps best remembered for ordering the murder of Thomas à Becket in 1170.

Henry II's sons Richard I and John inherited something from their Angevin ancestry, having violent tempers and a disposition, particularly in John, to extreme cruelty. St Bernard, the Cistercian abbot of Clairvaux in France, was to say of them, 'From the Devil they came and to the Devil they shall return.'[14]

It was believed that John had personally murdered his nephew, Arthur, who had been named as heir by Richard before embarking on a crusade to the Holy Land. The young man had been imprisoned first at Falaise and then at Rouen. On the Thursday before Easter, 3 April 1203, 'when he was drunk and possessed by the Devil', the King killed Arthur and sank his body, weighted with a stone, in the River Seine.[15] The story bears the stamp of truth, having been recorded by the chronicler of Margam Abbey in Glamorgan, who had it from William de Briouze, one of the abbey's patrons and the captor of Arthur at Mirebeau.[16]

Edward was born at Westminster Palace on 18 June 1239, the eldest son of Henry III. He succeeded to the throne on 16 November 1272, while in Palestine, and his thoughts as a dying man were to return to that time.[19]

In physical appearance he was a lean man of considerable height, seven feet in his armour,[18] in an age when men generally were of short stature,[19] thus giving rise to his nickname 'Edward Longshanks'. He was energetic and brave and possessed great stamina, even taking part in the Battle of Falkirk at the age of almost sixty, after an accident in which he was trampled by his horse.[20] He had inherited his father's drooping eyelid[21] and was said to have been clear and emphatic in speech, but the underlying malice in his character made him a dangerous adversary.

He married Eleanor of Castile in 1254, when she was ten

and he fifteen. She bore him sixteen children, of whom most were girls. His heir was his fourteenth child, born in the thirtieth year of his marriage.[22] The boy, born in Wales and raised by a Welsh nurse, was created Prince of Wales in 1301, a title since borne by all male heirs to the throne.[23]

Men who survive disasters tend to believe themselves untouchable by Fate, with a free hand to direct their own destinies. The death of his wife, Eleanor, from fever, on 25 November 1290, removed a restraining influence on Edward's activities. Thereafter he was to indulge in acts of horrifying destruction, as at Berwick in 1296, as well as the petty meannesses of a monarch whose word was the only law that mattered.

In 1283 he appropriated funds which had been collected for a new crusade to Palestine.[24] When John Pecham, the Archbishop of Canterbury, delivered the Pope's outraged demand for their return, Edward assumed an air of surprised innocence but, realizing his error in challenging papal authority quite so blatantly, he handed them back.

When in need of money in 1294, he threatened to deprive the clergy of his protection if they refused to give him one half of all clerical revenues. By September 1295, after endless bullying, some £80,000 had been collected and handed over.[25]

Among the many benefits he brought England was his successful reorganization of the wool trade, which was to become the country's most profitable export for centuries to come. He completed the judicial reforms begun by Henry III (r.1216–72), instituting separately appointed judges for the courts of King's Bench, Common Pleas and Exchequer. He also set up the Chancery Court, to give redress when other courts had failed.

Yet, having spent the winter of 1304 at Dunfermline Abbey, he could order it set on fire as he rode away, although it contained the tombs of his sister Margaret and her husband, Alexander III.[26] The banners of St Cuthbert and John of Beverley were carried at the head of his army, alongside the Plantagenet leopards of England.[27] Yet he turned the church of Saint Michael at Linlithgow into a grain store and ordered the lead stripped from the roofs of churches at Perth and Dunblane for his siege-engines.[28]

Nor must it be forgotten that he drove two countries which had been at peace for a hundred years to hatreds that were to leave a legacy of distrust and bitterness for centuries to come.[29]

Pactum Serva – 'Keep Faith' – is inscribed on Edward I's tomb in Westminster Abbey, but he used treaties and the law only as long as they benefited himself. He had no use for diplomacy. If Scotland would not accept him as overlord, his only answer was to invade it, with all the attendant miseries of war.

A letter from the Scottish nobles to the Pope in 1320 sums up Edward's role in Scotland's history: 'We continued to enjoy peace and liberty ... until Edward, the late King of England, in the guise of a friend and ally, invaded and oppressed our nation, at that time without a head, unpractised in war, and suspecting no evil.'[30]

The Scottish War of Independence began when Edward's fortunes were on the ascendant and Alexander III's had begun to run out.

5   *Toom Tabard*

A lamb in the midst of wolves.
Murison

In 1275 Alexander III's wife, Margaret, sister of Edward I, died, followed by a run of disasters which was to alter the future history of Scotland.

In 1280 his younger son, David, died, aged eight. In April 1283 his daughter, Margaret, wife of Eric, King of Norway, died. In 1284 his elder son, Alexander, followed. The male line of the Celtic kings of Scotland was now embodied in the Queen of Norway's one-year-old daughter, whom Alexander's council recognized as his heir on 5 February 1284.[1]

It was, however, a source of sharp anxiety to those in power that the succession rested on so unstable a foundation. There had been child monarchs before, and their accession had always aroused a fierce struggle for power among the foremost nobles. But no woman had ever before been the ruler of Scotland, and the universal hope was that Alexander, a vigorous man in good health, would take a second wife and give the country a male heir.

To their relief, in October 1285 Alexander married Yolande, or Joleta, daughter of the Count of Dreux.

The ceremony took place at Jedburgh Abbey, being followed by a pageant seen for the first time in Scotland. It is probable that Alexander's new wife planned to surprise and delight her husband with a masque familiar enough on the Continent and called 'the Dance of Death'.[2] While masked dancers gambolled before the royal couple, Death in the guise of a skeleton made a dramatic appearance and pretended to strike terror in the performers. It had a similar effect on the scandalized guests, who regarded the performance as wholly unsuitable for a celebration of marriage. Their gloomy forebodings that ill fortune would follow all too rapidly came true.

On a stormy 19 March 1286, Alexander attended a council in Edinburgh Castle.[3] Although the hour was late before he could get away, he insisted on returning to his young queen at Kinghorn in Fife. The ferrymaster at Dalmeny endeavoured to dissuade him from undertaking the crossing to Inverkeithing, two miles distant, but Alexander demanded impatiently to be rowed across the turbulent River Forth. Once he had landed on the other side, two local men were enlisted to guide the King through the darkness in the ferocious gale, and the party set off. At some time thereafter, Alexander became separated from the others. His horse stumbled over a cliff and plunged the 44-year-old King to his death.[4]

Scarcely had Alexander been buried than old rivalries sprang up. In the north were the Comyns, in the south was the elderly Robert Bruce, Lord of Annandale. Between them, with a precarious hold on both life and the Scottish throne, was the infant Margaret, called 'the Maid of Norway' and 'the Damsel of Scotland'.[5]

It was essential to appoint a regency, and this was formed on 11 April 1286, with three nobles from the north and three from the south of the country: the Earls of Buchan and Fife, the Bishops of St Andrews and Glasgow, and two barons, James the Steward and John Comyn of Badenoch.[6]

The decision to exclude him from the council infuriated Robert Bruce, Lord of Annandale and ex-Chief Justice of England, who considered himself to have an inviolate right to the Scottish throne.

On 9 March 1238 Alexander II's queen, Joanna, sister of Henry III, had died without issue. To safeguard the succession, the King named Robert Bruce, sometimes called 'the Competitor', as heir presumptive. Bruce was the son of Alexander's cousin Isabel and was unanimously accepted as the King's heir by the nobles.[7]

However, in May 1239 Alexander remarried, and his wife, Marie de Coucy, daughter of a French nobleman, bore him a son in September 1241, who was to become Alexander III.[8]

This new closeness to France had alarmed Henry III to the extent that he closed English and Irish ports to Scottish shipping and barricaded the roads into England.[9] However, after meeting Alexander at Newcastle on 1 August 1244, a fresh treaty was agreed, whereby the Scottish King gave his word not to enter into any alliance which would affect the safety of England.

The family of de Brus was one of an élite group of barons in Scotland in the Middle Ages. Their forebear, Adam de Brus, had come over with the Conqueror in 1066, and in 1124 was granted the lordship of Annandale and 200,000 acres straddling the important western route between England and Scotland.[10] Their lands included the strategic castles of Lochmaben, at the head of the Annandale valley, and Carlaverock.

In May 1240 Robert the Competitor married Isobel de Clare, daughter of the Earl of Gloucester, and niece of the Earl Marshal of England, and continued to be highly regarded by Henry III, whom he served loyally.[11]

His second wife, whom he married in May 1273, was Christiana of Ireby.[12] Robert and Isobel's son, Robert, born in 1253, married Marjory, Countess of Carrick, and became Earl of Carrick in her right.

It is certain, however, that the Competitor never for one moment forgot that he had once stood as close to the Scottish throne as was possible and that he might yet acquire the crown if Fate decreed it. It requires little imagination to accept that the Competitor's son, the Earl of Carrick, and his grandson, also named Robert Bruce, grew up with a sense of irrevocable right to rule Scotland.

Smarting from his exclusion from the regency, Bruce the Competitor raised his vassals and, with his son, seized the royal strongholds in the west: Dumfries Castle, Wigton Castle and the Balliol stronghold of Buittle.[13] However, on hearing that the new Guardians had received Edward's royal approval, he backed off from open conflict.

There is some evidence that Bruce made a pact at this

time with a number of adherents.[14] On 20 September 1286 Patrick, Earl of Dunbar, and his three sons, the Earl of Menteith, James the Steward, who had been made one of the Guardians, his brother John, and Angus, son of Donald of the Isles, agreed to lend their support to Richard de Burgh, Earl of Ulster, and Lord Thomas de Clare, who was a brother of Edward's son-in-law and also brother-in-law to Bruce. It is not known what the bond entailed, but it was certainly connected with an intended later bid by the Competitor for the throne.

For four years the regency worked well. By 1289, however, the Earl of Buchan had died of old age and the Earl of Fife had been murdered by his kinsmen.[15] Those remaining Guardians – Comyn, James Stewart and the two bishops – were well aware that the Lord of Annandale remained restive in his eastern stronghold and was still intent on seizing power.

In the same year, Eric of Norway sent envoys to England concerning his daughter's future. Edward was determined to bring about a marriage between the little Queen Margaret and his son, aged five.[16] The Scots Council had agreed in principle, although the children were cousins and thus within the prohibited degrees. Edward, however, had sent Sir Otto de Grandison to Rome, to obtain a dispensation from Pope Nicholas IV that would enable the union to take place.[17] All seemed set fair for a continuation of friendly and peaceful relations between the two countries, soon to be allied by a royal marriage.

During April and May 1289, envoys sailed between England and Norway, endeavouring to hasten the Norwegian King into making a decision. Edward took pains to point out how unsettled the situation remained in Scotland and that, from the child's point of view, her only safety lay in the security of England.

Finally, on 6 November 1289, representatives of the three countries met at Salisbury to sign a treaty, by which Eric would send the Maid to Scotland by 1 November of the following year. To induce him to keep to his bargain, he was made a substantial loan of 2,000 marks by Edward, with particularly easy terms for repayment.[18]

Eric, however, continued to drag his heels, despite a ship's being fitted out at Yarmouth in Norfolk, which took forty days to prepare.[19] At last, on 9 May Antony Bek, the Bishop of Durham, sailed from Hartlepool for Norway, bearing gifts for the little Queen. Bek was a skilful diplomat and made a point of distributing largesse to various Norwegian officials who might help influence Eric's mind. They were to receive £400 a year until the Queen reached the age of fifteen – a considerable and no doubt gratefully received sum of money.[20] Bek and the ship, however, returned empty-handed.[21]

Edward now began to assume powers over Scottish affairs that alarmed the regency. He would, of course, become father-in-law to Queen Margaret on her marriage, but he now acted as though all decisions concerning Scotland were his responsibility alone. It was a matter of urgency that matters be put down in black and white regarding the extent of English influence in Scotland.

On 18 July 1290, at the signing of the Treaty of Birgham, it was agreed that Scotland would remain separate from, and entirely independent of, England.[22] No vassal of the Scottish Crown would do homage for his Scottish lands in England; all offices of state were to be held by Scots, and no subject would be answerable at law outside the kingdom. In addition, Church matters would be free of interference by England.[23]

While the Scottish council had been discussing the treaty, without having reached the point of signing it, Edward sent an armed force under Walter Huntercomb which, on 4 June 1290, seized the Isle of Man.[24] This action threw the Scots commissioners into a state of confusion and alarm, which increased when Edward followed it up by demanding that all Scottish fortifications be placed in his hands.

This the Scots indignantly refused to consider. Edward's response was to send the Bishop of Durham, negotiator of the treaty, to Scotland as his representative on behalf of the young Queen, his ruling in all matters concerning the government to be accepted without argument. The two bishops in the regency being pro-English, with Bek's appointment the balance of power shifted at once in Edward's favour. The Treaty of Birgham was ratified on 28 August 1290, at Northampton, but the Scots undoubtedly went home with grave doubts about its future effectiveness.

Undoubtedly Edward was kept informed by spies of the unlikelihood of the Maid's surviving into adulthood. Information that she was delicate must have given him a glow of anticipation, for a country divided by ambitious nobles seeking power in the absence of a strong ruler was one that much more likely to fall prey to himself.

In 1291 he informed his privy council that, 'He had it in his mind to bring under his dominion the King and the realm of Scotland, in the same manner that he had subdued the Kingdom of Wales'.[25] In 1282 Prince Llewelyn of Wales had been defeated and killed in battle, after which Wales was annexed to the English Crown. It remained, however, outside the kingdom and was not granted representation in parliament.[26]

One might describe Edward's determination to subjugate Scotland as the obsession of a man who could not stand to be thwarted. Instead of aiming at a peaceful relationship with a country that had no wish to be driven to war in order to retain its independence, year after year, from 1297 until his death in 1307, he raised an army that burned, destroyed and ravaged Scotland.

The opportunity for placing Scotland firmly in his power came in September 1290. The child Queen had finally sailed for Scotland, and Bek had been sent to meet her ship in Orkney with gifts of jewels. The little girl, however, died either before reaching land or soon after, around the end of September.[27]

There are no details of her death, but a curious footnote of history survives in the claims in 1301 of a young woman to be Margaret, relating how she had been abducted in the Orkneys on the voyage to Scotland and spirited away. The unfortunate girl was burned at the stake in Bergen as an impostor.[28]

The death of the child Queen made the appointment of an immediate successor essential if the country were not to slide into civil war. Already there were three – and later thirteen – claimants, all ambitious for the throne, with some prepared to back their claims, if necessary, by an armed offensive. The Norman-descended Bishop of St Andrews, William Fraser, now took a step that was to have fateful consequences for Scotland. Of his own volition, he wrote privately to Edward on 7 October 1290, inviting him to come north and judge the merits of the individual claimants.[29] In addition, most alarmingly, Robert Bruce of Annandale had arrived in Perth with an army of supporters who included the Earls of Mar and Atholl, and appeared to be making a bid to seize the throne for himself.[30]

It is said that the Bishop took the opportunity of recommending that Edward look favourably on John Balliol, a man he was certain would prove amenable to the King's intentions.[31]

Edward at once blandly agreed to be adviser for the succession and during the winter invited all religious houses to search their chronicles for entries concerning relations between the two countries.[32] By 10 May 1291 some had responded, and these he presented to a parliament of Scots nobles and clergy summoned at Norham, near the Bishop of Durham's castle. The Bishop of Bath and Wells, Chancellor of England, assured Edward that, from earliest times, the English king had always held the overlordship of Scotland. Edward, therefore, was justified in maintaining that he was fully entitled to decide the rights of the various claimants and must be regarded in future as Lord Paramount of Scotland.[33]

Thrown into confusion by this blunt statement, the Scots requested time to consider. Edward granted them nine days, which was extended after protest to three weeks, none of them wasted by the King.[34] The English army marched north and was a day away from the Scottish borders when Edward again met the regents, this time in the village of Upsetlington, on the north bank of the River Tweed and thus on Scottish soil. Eight of the claimants were present, and all formally acknowledged Edward as their Lord Superior. The day following, John Balliol took a similar oath.[35]

The claimants were, of course, vassals of Edward and owed him their estates in England, many of them vast and of considerably greater value than those in Scotland. To have stood out against him then would have resulted in an armed confrontation with the might of England, and a certain loss of their wealth and position.

On 11 June 1291 Edward ordered that every Scottish castle be turned over to him until two months after the succession was decided, and that all Scots officials be replaced by English.[36] He then proceeded to make a progress as far as Perth, every class being required to pay him homage, all who refused being arrested and held until they did.[37]

On 3 August 1291 Edward met the Scots council once more, this time at Berwick. Although twelve claimants were present – Eric of Norway would later become the thirteenth[38] – only three could be seriously considered: John Balliol, Robert Bruce and John Hastings, and of these, from a legal angle, the rightful heir was Balliol.

John Balliol was the grandson of the eldest daughter of David, Earl of Huntingdon, the brother of William the Lyon (r.1165–1214). Bruce was the son of the second daughter, and Hastings the grandson of the third.[39]

Balliol was married to the daughter of John de Warenne, Earl of Surrey, one of Edward's most able generals, and was the son of the founder of Balliol College, Oxford.[40] He had few ties with Scotland but owned large estates in France, where he spent much of his time, as well as others in Northumberland and Durham. Balliol's sister, Alianora, was the wife of John Comyn, one of the Scottish Guardians. Their son, John Comyn 'the Red', was to be murdered by Bruce in 1306.

Balliol possessed rather delicate features and deep-set eyes and was, perhaps, more intelligent than people realized. He was unfailingly courteous and too forbearing ever to take a stand against a man of Edward's steely nature.

Because of their kinship with Balliol, the powerful Comyn family, if they could not achieve succession for themselves, were ready to back him strongly. Ranged against them was the elderly Bruce, totally opposed to seeing his rivals given power, and still believing he had prior right to the throne.

The proceedings meandered on, the delay suiting Edward well, for the longer Scotland lacked a stable government, the better the chance of internal discord's disrupting the country's running and its annexation to himself.

On 17 November 1292 Edward declared that, in both English and Scottish law, the rightful heir was Balliol.[41] As a token of England's superiority, the Great Seal which had been used by the regents since the death of Alexander III was broken in pieces and sent to the English treasury. On the following day, Balliol swore an oath of allegiance to Edward, his Lord Superior, and he was crowned at Scone on 30 November 1292.

Bruce the Competitor, who was in his eighties, quietly left the political arena and retired to his estates, where he died on 1 April 1295.

His son, the Earl of Carrick, deciding not to compromise his claim to the throne, made over his earldom to his 17-year-old son, young Bruce, the future king, on 7 November 1291.[42] He then sailed with his eldest daughter, Isobel, for Norway, where he made a lengthy stay. A year later she became Queen of Norway on her marriage to Eric.[43]

On Carrick's return, after his father's death, he was appointed governor of Carlisle Castle, in October 1295, and remained as such until October 1297.[44] Edward then dismissed him, due to young Bruce's suspect loyalty to himself, after which Carrick retired to his estates and died in 1304.

The Competitor's grandson took himself off as well, to his Essex estates. While at the English Court, he married Isabella, daughter of the tenth Earl of Mar, who bore him a daughter, Marjory.

In 1315 the son of James the Steward was to marry Marjory. On 2 March 1316, while out riding, she was thrown from her horse and killed. Surgeons hurriedly summoned performed a caesarian operation and delivered a live son who was to become Robert II, the first

King of the House of Stuart.[45]

Well pleased with the outcome of his machinations, Edward returned to England, but Balliol's troubles were only beginning. An amiable man, he found himself unable to handle the fierce Scottish nobles, each of them determined to win a greater share of power for himself. Time and again he was summoned to England on some trifling matter or other by Edward, and only a month after his accession he found himself locked in serious conflict with the English King.[46]

Roger Bartholomew, a burgess of Berwick, having lost his triple lawsuit in the court of the Scottish Guardians, appealed to Edward on the grounds that he had been treated unjustly. By the Treaty of Birgham, 1290, it had been agreed that all Scottish law cases would be determined in Scotland; now Edward declared that he considered that the treaty had ended with Balliol's accession, and that he himself had the right to judge every Scottish lawsuit brought before him.

The Bartholomew case has an air of contrivance so early in Balliol's reign, and it is likely that it was intended to demonstrate to Balliol – and the Scots – who held power in Scotland.

Although John Comyn, Earl of Buchan, and the Bishop of St Andrews, with other prominent supporters, petitioned Edward to keep to the terms of the treaty, his reply was that it had applied only during the Interregnum. On 2 January 1293 he extracted Balliol's agreement that it was indeed null and void.[47]

Now followed a second case of appeal in which Balliol fared no better.

On the death of Malcolm, Earl of Fife, in 1266, his heir was an infant. The Earl's brother, Macduff, at once demanded part of the estate.[48] On having his claim dismissed by the Bishop of St Andrews, he appealed to Edward during the time of the Interregnum. The King ordered that Macduff's claims be tried by the regents, who decided in his favour. However, after a council held by Balliol at Scone, Macduff was once more dispossessed and, moreover, imprisoned for breaking the law. On his release, he appealed a second time to Edward, who ordered Balliol to appear before him on 25 March 1293 with an explanation.

Balliol, possibly stiffened by his nobles, refused, but a second demand followed, requiring his presence on 14 October 1293. To have failed to appear would have been equivalent to a declaration of war, and Balliol yielded. He was humiliatingly ordered to pay Macduff damages and hand over three important castles, Berwick, Roxburgh and Jedburgh, and their towns, to Edward.[49] Balliol protested as vigorously as a man of his nature could, and Edward, with apparent magnanimity, postponed the matter for a year.[50]

Before long, Balliol's nickname became 'Toom Tabard' – 'empty coat' – for his lack of resistance to Edward, and the hollowness of his position as monarch.

His reign as King John continued to stumble from one crisis to another, always at the prompting of the self-proclaimed Lord Superior of Scotland.

In 1290 Edward had banished 16,000 Jews, on the ground of extortionate usury, having earlier hanged 280 for money-clipping and forgery.[51] In the Middle Ages, the profession of money-lender was forbidden to Christians. When kings needed to finance foreign wars, they were obliged to obtain their funding from Jews, which accounted in large part for their acceptance in England at the time.

In May 1294, with Scotland satisfactorily under his thumb, Edward was planning an invasion of Gascony for which troops, and the means to pay them, were urgently required. Balliol was fetched down from Scotland and told to raise both. On his reporting back to his council at Scone, their reaction was one of fury. An immediate decision was made to expel all Englishmen from the Court, their lands in Scotland to be forfeited.[52]

Bruce was among those dispossessed, his Annandale estates being handed over to his bitterest enemy, John Comyn, Earl of Buchan, in an act designed to intensify their feud.[53]

A standing committee of twelve was set up, consisting of earls, barons and bishops, to administer the country's affairs, the Scots finally realizing that they could place no confidence in Balliol's ability to rule.[54]

A further important step was also taken. In 1295 a secret alliance was concluded between Scotland and France, by which Balliol's son would marry King Philip's niece, Jeanne de Valois, the eldest daughter of Charles, Count of Valois and Anjou.[55] It was not the first time that France and Scotland had become allies against England, but this treaty in particular would still carry importance 400 years later, during the Jacobite Rebellions of 1715 and 1745, when Scotland still sought independence from English rule.

Confident, no doubt, that Edward would presently sail for France with his army, on 26 March 1296 Comyn, Earl of Buchan, mustered an army and led it south into Cumberland.[56] Intent on demonstrating to Edward that England had meddled for the last time in Scottish affairs, this ill-judged invasion was to have disastrous results which were to overshadow every other event in Edward's reign, and lead directly to the rise of William Wallace as his country's champion of liberty.

6   The Making of an Outlaw

A certain public robber.
Hemingburgh

It must again be emphasized that we are dependent on Blind Harry for stories of Wallace's activities in the years 1292 to 1296. Nevertheless, the minstrel grew up at a time when tales of his hero's exploits were still being handed down to each new generation, originating from men who had fought with him, or families who had given him shelter and support.

The enormous upheavals that took place in 1297 were enshrined in the hearts and memories of thousands of Scots men and women. No one in Scotland remained untouched by them. The Scottish Church regained its power; towns whose castles had been occupied by foreign troops saw them driven out; hated officials, such as tax-gatherers and judges, were sent fleeing for safety to England. Scotland became an armed camp, and tales of that exciting, triumphant and, for Wallace, ultimately disastrous time, when he rallied the nation behind him, must have been repeated down the years very much as they had happened.

If Harry erred in some of his details, this is not to say that the basic facts were false. Everything Wallace had done for his country, in giving it first hope and then an active resistance to a foreign occupation, with its attendant cruelties and injustice, was remembered with affection and pride and used as an inspiration for children growing up in a freedom made possible by his courage.

Certainly Wallace did not appear suddenly, as the commander of an army of 10,000 men at Stirling Bridge in September 1297, an inspired leader with no previous combat experience behind him. There must have been a period of preparation for a victory that overwhelmed an experienced English force, and it is to Harry that we must turn for tales of these early years. Battle skills have, after all, to be learned; tactics have to be mastered; the elements of command and delegation become second nature under intense pressure. Wallace was more than a mere guerrilla leader, although he was always at his most successful in fast, close combat attacks, where speed and initiative gave him the advantage over armoured heavy horse. He was, in fact, a born soldier, inspired by a passionate desire to free his countrymen from English rule, which gave him reserves of fortitude and determination.

All the exploits Harry records of the time in question involve Sir Henry de Percy, the Warden of Galloway and Ayr, who was appointed on 8 September 1296, although he did not take up his post until late October. If, however, the name of the man who was the official had escaped Harry's memory, he may well have used 'Percy' as representing English authority.

Sir Reginald Crauford, who had taken an oath of allegiance and been confirmed as Sheriff of Ayr, offered to have the outlawry of his hot-headed young nephew quashed, but Wallace scorned to accept.[1] It was a matter of pride that he should be so regarded by the English, and he would not abase himself in order to assume the rights of a free man again. Before long, however, he became involved in an incident which made academic his uncle's attempts to help him.

While Wallace was idling away his time at Riccarton, fishing in the Water of Irvine, a group of Percy's attendants appeared. They proceeded to help themselves to Wallace's catch, whereupon he started up and either killed or injured three of them before making his escape.[2]

Sir Richard Wallace must have been thoroughly dismayed at his nephew's fresh incursion into violence against the English, and he was dispatched post-haste to another relative, Wallace of Auchincruive. There he was concealed in nearby Laglane Wood and supplied with food until the furore died down.[3]

However, Wallace could not content himself in inactivity and decided to take a look at nearby Ayr, a busy market town garrisoned by English troops. It was, of course, an act of the most foolhardy, but one which delighted the young man with its daring.

Among the entertainers in the market-place was a local champion, offering to let anyone give him a blow from a bucket-pole on payment of a groat – a painful way, one would have said, of earning a living. Wallace handed him three groats, gave the fellow a tremendous wallop and sent him sprawling.[4] A number of soldiers on duty, delegated to keep order on market day, on hearing the uproar at once made for Wallace, and in the ensuing fight several were killed.

The excitement at seeing a lone Scotsman taking on a troop of English soldiers must have set the rooftops of Ayr ringing. Heads would appear at windows, catcalls and cheers resound, the braver would take the opportunity of pelting the English with refuse, and in the midst of it, Wallace would be dashing for the edge of the wood where he had left his horse, and vanishing before a pursuit could be organized.

The exploit had been witnessed in a crowded market-place and carried by word of mouth before the day was over. The talk of the alehouses, the gossip conveyed by pedlars and carters to the next town, must soon have identified the tall, good-looking young man as William Wallace of Elderslie. The realization that a flame of rebellion still burned in a people bullied into submission by Edward of England must have spread with joyous rapidity.

A second story related by Harry, also over a matter of fish, may refer to one and the same episode.[5] Sir Reginald's servant, having bought fish at Ayr market, had his produce insultingly demanded by Percy's steward. Wallace protested, whereupon the steward lashed out at him with his staff. Wallace's response was to seize him and stab him dead.

This time there were eighty soldiers on duty, who captured Wallace after a fierce struggle and threw him in prison. Suffering from injuries received in the fight and otherwise badly treated, Wallace became so ill that, when the time came for him to be brought up for sentencing, the gaoler found him to all appearances moribund. His old nurse, living in the New Town of Ayr, asked permission to collect the body for burial and had it conveyed to her house.[6]

One may see behind this tale the unseen presence of Wallace's friends, bribed gaolers and the discreet part played by such men as Sir Reginald Crauford and Sir Richard Wallace. Keeping up the pretence that Wallace was dead, his nurse tended him until he had completely recovered.

About this time, 'True Thomas the Rimer' – Sir Thomas Rymour of Erceldoune (c. 1220–97) – was paying a visit to the nearby monastery of St Mary's at Faile, which had the reputation of owning an excellent wine cellar.[7] In 1286 he was said to have foretold the death of Alexander II.[8] In consequence, his prophecies were listened to with respect.

The monks had certainly heard of Wallace's exploits at Ayr, which were in turn related to True Thomas. The celebrated seer expressed such concern that one of their number was sent to discover Wallace's fate. On hearing that the reports of the young man's death were false, Thomas declared:

> For sooth, ere he decease,
> Shall many thousands in the field make end.
> From Scotland he shall forth the Southern send,
> And Scotland thrice he shall bring to the peace.
> So good of hand again shall ne'er be kenned.[9]

This prediction by so renowned a personality, that Wallace would drive the English out of Scotland, passed rapidly beyond the walls of St Mary's, to such an extent that the English authorities became seriously concerned.[10]

Nor must the effect these words had on Wallace himself be overlooked, for they occurred at a time when his mind had become receptive to the promptings of Fate.

Up to then, his attacks on the English had been carried

out very much single-handedly. His temper had fired up and he had taken a quick personal revenge. Now, in the inactivity forced on him by his convalescence, Wallace must have found himself giving slow and steady thought to True Thomas's words.

Could he possibly be the one to arouse his country to a resistance that would sweep the enemy out of Scotland? Was Destiny pointing a finger in his direction in a sign that carried with it the awesome responsibility of leading an entire nation against the power of England?

He was a young man, without fortune or great estates. He lacked friends in positions of influence. He had never commanded so much as a group of friends in an attack on trained soldiers, and knew nothing of battle tactics beyond the most elementary.

What he did have was a deep and abiding resentment of the tyrants who assumed themselves to be the masters of his country, and a passionate desire to free Scotland to its rightful king. Could he direct these emotions in such a way that they inspired his countrymen to rise as an army? If so, his resistance to the occupying forces must alter. No longer could he hit out at this or that group of local soldiery. His horizons must widen to embrace the whole of his country's ability to raise up a fighting force of men who thought as he did and who were willing to put their trust in his leadership.

Many of his young kinsmen, second or third sons with no hope of inheritance, were already sympathetic to his views. Then there were the friends he had made at Dundee, as well as older relatives in positions of modest power, who might lend him a discreet support. His heart must have beat faster as he realized he already had a nucleus of recruits, waiting only to be directed by a man with a bold enough vision to lead them.

If there was, indeed, a point at which Wallace took on the mantle of his country's deliverer, when freedom from English rule became all at once a practical possibility, provided he had the courage to stand forth and declare himself by deeds not yet accomplished but already forming in his imagination, perhaps that was the moment when he swore never to rest until he had swept the

English out of Scotland and reinstated its independence.

Spirited away from Ayr by his relatives, Wallace had by now accepted that he lacked the temperament to skulk in Laglane Wood, continually forcing his kinsmen to place their lives at risk by giving him shelter and support. He had already formulated plans for his future, and almost at once the opportunity presented itself to put them into action.

He had never forgotten the name of the English officer responsible for his father's death, and it is likely that sympathizers kept him informed of Fenwick's movements. The chance for revenge now arose, when he learned that a convoy in the charge of Fenwick was *en route* along the Western Marches from Carlisle to Ayr.

Such movements of stores were always well guarded, for Galloway was in a state of more or less permanent unrest, and wagons and pack-horses carrying arms and provisions were a temptation to robbers. Fenwick had 180 men with him, some of them reinforcements for Ayr Castle.

It says much for Wallace's new confidence that he found himself with fifty friends and kinsmen at his side at Loudon Hill, all committed to whatever action he intended to carry out.[11] These included Adam Wallace, now aged eighteen, young Sir Robert Boyd, later comrade to Bruce, Kneland, Edward Little, Gray and Kerby.

It was now that Wallace was to display his skill in those guerrilla tactics which were to make him famous. He ordered a rough dyke of boulders constructed across the narrow track, as though there had been an earth fall, leaving just enough room for one rider at a time. As the English troops arrived and milled about in an effort to get by, Wallace's men leapt from their cover and attacked in close order.[12] Using spears, knives and swords, they killed or wounded a hundred of the enemy. Wallace struck Fenwick from his horse, and he was killed by Robert Boyd. The remaining soldiers fled on horseback, abandoning the pack animals with their valuable booty. This was carried off into the forest of Clydesdale and shared out among sympathizers.[13]

An exploit of this nature could not be hushed up. Before long, men were repeating True Thomas's prophecy and looking hopefully towards the young man who, it had been promised, would rid their country of the usurper. The myth of the invincibility of heavily armoured troops on horseback had been destroyed by Wallace's daring attack, in which, thanks to his imaginative use of natural resources, lightly armed, untrained men were the victors.[14]

This action of Wallace's bears the stamp of truth. He is not made personally to dispatch Fenwick, as might be expected of an invincible hero, the honour going instead to an 18-year-old cousin.

The numbers of those killed in such affrays, as given by Harry, must always be considered with caution, but that a superior number of trained soldiers were scattered in a rout, leaving some at least of their companions dead or dying, can well be accepted.

The incident had immediate repercussions for Wallace's long-suffering uncle, Sir Reginald Crauford, who was summoned for a second time to a council in Glasgow, where he was expected to give recognisances for his nephew's future good behaviour.[15] Possibly the English authorities had determined to lay hands on Wallace, once he was safely out of Riccarton land, and to deal with him rigorously, for Sir Percy and a number of his attendants arrived to escort both men. Accompanying Wallace were two of his kinsmen, Gray and Kerby.

Somewhere on the journey, Percy's horse faltered, and his chief steward rode back to demand that Sir Reginald exchange his own, fresher mount for Sir Percy's. To Wallace, this must have been a clear indication of what awaited his uncle in Glasgow. If a servant could treat Sir Reginald with such insolence, the latter was probably in danger of losing his position as Sheriff of Ayr, or at least of being heavily fined for his nephew's misdeeds.

Sir Reginald, anxious not to stir up fresh trouble, expressed his willingness to dismount. Wallace, incensed, galloped off with Gray and Kerby and presently left the convoy behind. Ahead of them, near Cathcart, they came on Percy's baggage train. Leaving its five guards either dead or wounded, Wallace and his friends drove off the wagons and had vanished before Percy reached the spot.[16]

The council promptly outlawed Wallace once again.[17] This had the effect of calling even greater attention to his exploits, for Wallace was engaging in extremely daring attacks on the authority of England that delighted his countrymen. It is certain that reports were sent to England about this young brigand. King Edward, however, was busy with preparations for the war in Flanders and had not yet realized that these events were the forerunner of something far more threatening than purely local disturbances.

What occurred now was that men began to flock to Wallace, outlaws from Selkirk Forest, landless men, the younger sons of knights, Irish exiles – what man would come to him, Wallace welcomed.[18]

Whether or not Harry's tales are completely accurate, it is obvious that during these formative years Wallace was certainly doing something about the English occupation that reached the King's ears. Possibly from this period comes an undated document which states that Edward de Keith is granted 'all goods and chattels of whatever kind he may gain from Messire William le Waleys the King's enemy'.[19]

It was now Easter, 26 March 1296. In the west, Comyn, Earl of Buchan, was leading his army over the Borders into Cumberland, determined to demonstrate that England meddled with Scotland at its peril. If he had heard of Wallace's activities, he was likely to have dismissed them as the actions of a local hothead. Sweeping south with the intention of taking Carlisle, he rode through Annandale and those lands that had so recently belonged to Robert Bruce.

Other nobles, such as the Earls of Angus and Dunbar, had decided to remain aloof from this foolhardy enterprise into England, and had in consequence been deprived of their Scottish estates by King John Balliol.[20]

At Carlisle, however, Comyn came up against opponents who were not prepared to yield. These were Bruce of Annandale and his son, the young Earl of Carrick, who together with the citizenry barred the gates to the Scots army.[21] It is unlikely that, even had their enemy, Comyn, not been in command, Bruce and his son would have acted any differently. They had given oaths of allegiance to Edward which they intended to hold, at least for the time being. Young Bruce was often to be accused of changing sides when it suited him, or of sitting on the fence until he saw which side would win, but in this instance he acted with a good deal of cool foresight. He and his father were not against Scotland but against Comyn's power increasing through his kinsman, Balliol.

Frustrated by their inability to take Carlisle, the Scots burned part of the town and turned west into Northumberland, carrying out a great deal of pointless destruction, looting and burning churches, monasteries and villages in Corbridge, Hexham and Lanercost.

By now, it was apparent to Edward that these minor disorders were rapidly becoming a war, and he marched north with an army. It must have amused him to discover that his lapdog, Balliol, had suddenly developed teeth.

On Good Friday, 30 March 1296, Edward, with 30,000 soldiers and 5,000 mounted men, arrived at Berwick, the largest and most prosperous town in Scotland. The amount of £2,000 taken at its Customs was one quarter of the entire sum raised in ports of England.[22] Merchantmen carried trade back and forth to the Continent, and it shared with Inverness the important industry of shipbuilding.

On 23 February, a month earlier, several English traders had been killed at Berwick and their goods stolen, in one of those flash-flood upsurges of resentment against the English occupation.[23] Whether or not Edward learned of this is unknown, but on the presumption that he did and that he considered it an affront to his personal power, he determined to take a revenge on Berwick so terrible that it has remained one of the most horrifying actions of his reign.

From his camp at Hutton, the King rode to the gates of the town and ordered its citizens to surrender. Their response was to jeer at Edward and defy him to do his worst.[24]

The town was surrounded by an earth-and-wood rampart which it was obvious, as the English army came in sight, was going to provide little defence against cavalry. However, the cry went up from the garrison, which comprised men from Fife, that the banners to be seen were those of nobles on Balliol's side and that the approaching army was not English but Scots.

In this they were disastrously mistaken. It is said that Edward had employed the same stratagem at the Battle of Evesham in June 1265.[25] At Evesham, he had the banners captured from Montfort's army at Kenilworth carried ahead of his troops, thus lulling his opponents into believing that their allies approached. At a given moment, the captured flags were thrown aside, to be replaced by the leopards of England. By the time the mistake was realized, the opposing force was hopelessly confused and put to rout.

This now happened at Berwick, where possibly the garrison failed to realize that Bruce of Annandale and his son, the Earl of Carrick, were on the side of the enemy.[26] Before Berwick's citizens could organize any sort of resistance, their defences were smashed down by Edward's cavalry, and the English were pouring into the town.

A group of thirty Flemish craftsmen took refuge in the Guildhall, called the Red Hall and put up a gallant fight. An arrow shot from this building struck the King's cousin, Richard of Cornwall, through the eyeslit of his helmet and killed him instantly.[27] Enraged, Edward issued that most terrible of orders: *no quarter*.

The Red Hall was set on fire, and all its defenders perished.[28] Men, women, children and babies were put to the sword amid scenes of frightful carnage. The butchery continued for three days, during which time Sir William Douglas, governor of the castle, appalled at the mindless killing going on in the town, surrendered to Edward. It is said that, only when Edward saw a woman giving birth to a child as she was hacked to death by an English soldier did the King finally respond to the pleading of his religious advisers and call a halt.[29]

Berwick never recovered its former importance.[30] The

dead were so numerous, and the risk of pestilence was so acute, that they were dumped in their hundreds into hurriedly dug pits or thrown into the sea. Various estimates are given as to the number who perished, possibly as many as 17,000 – Matthew of Westminster put the figure at 60,000[31] – in an event which makes one of the most shameful pages in English history.

As though to conceal the effects of what had taken place, Edward set about the rapid refortification of the devastated town, even undertaking some of the labouring work himself.[32]

The sack of Berwick sent shock-waves of horror throughout Scotland as the news spread.

'From this time,' says Pearson, 'a sea of blood lay between the English King and his Scottish dominion,' and the conduct of the war altered to one of deepest hatred on the part of Scotland of all things English, and a detestation of Edward.[33]

On 5 April 1296 the Abbot of Arbroath brought a letter from Balliol, renouncing his allegiance to Edward.

'What folly he commits!' exclaimed Edward grimly. 'If he will not come to us, we will go to him.'[34]

The Scots, under the Earl of Buchan, then carried out a revenge attack, ravaging Redesdale, Cockermouth and Tyndale, and the monastery of Hexham.[35] But on hearing rumours of Edward's approach, they fled back to Scotland.

Spies now brought Edward news that another force of Scots had seized Earl Patrick's castle of Dunbar. He at once sent the experienced Warenne to deal with the situation, while the castle's Scottish defenders sent an urgent appeal for help to Balliol. On 27 April 1296 the Scottish army responded and took up a position on the slopes of the Lammermoor Hills, at Spottsmuir, near Dunbar.[36]

The result of the ensuing battle was total defeat for the Scots. Believing that the English forces were retreating, as they watched them break into groups to cross the valley that separated the two armies, they rushed downwards to speed them on their way. But their cries of derision fumbled into silence as Edward's better-disciplined, battle-hardened Flanders veterans re-formed and charged. One hundred and thirty important knights were captured, with the Earls of Menteith, Atholl and Ross, and sent as prisoners to England.[37] Next day, Dunbar Castle surrendered.

This débâcle thus deprived Scotland of her most experienced leaders and left her army without direction or commander. Roxburgh Castle surrendered on 8 May, followed by Jedburgh two weeks later and then Dumbarton. Edinburgh held out for several days before yielding, but when Edward reached Stirling Castle he found it abandoned by its garrison.[38]

There was no hope now that Balliol could hold on to his throne. Those of his advisers who were not prisoners in England were rapidly distancing themselves from him. On 7 July 1296, at Stracathro, he made a half-hearted gesture by renewing his treaty with France, but on 10 July, at Brechin, he renounced his kingdom to Edward's representative, the Bishop of Durham.[39] Scotland was now to be without a monarch for the next ten years.

Balliol appeared before Bek wearing a white robe, stripped of kingly ornaments and carrying the white rod of a penitent. Placing his baton and staff of office in Bek's hands, he formally renounced all claim to the kingdom of Scotland.[40]

In sending Balliol with his young son, Edward, to England by sea, the King acted leniently, well satisfied that events had transpired much as he had anticipated.

For three years Balliol remained technically a prisoner at Hertford, being restricted to an area within twenty miles of London. He was allowed a huntsman, a page and ten hounds, and given permission to hunt in any of Edward's forests south of the Trent.[41] When Wallace rose in Balliol's name in 1297, the latter and his son were housed for a time in the Tower, but on 18 July 1299 they were permitted to leave England under papal safeguards and delivered to the Bishop of Vicenza.[42] Eventually Balliol retired to his family estates at Bailleau,[43] where he lived quietly until his death in 1315, having survived long enough to learn of Bruce's victory at Bannockburn the previous year.[44]

Some measure of the lightness of his imprisonment may be taken from the fact that, when his luggage was searched before departure from Dover, a quantity of money and plate was found in it. This he was permitted to take with him, but the Scottish seal and a golden coronet he had contrived to keep hidden until then were confiscated.

Meanwhile, from Stirling, Edward continued his triumphant progress through Aberdeen and Banff as far as Elgin, the nobles hastening to offer him their allegiance and forswear their French alliance, before he turned for home.

At Scone he removed the Stone of Destiny on which every Celtic king had been crowned, and sent it to Westminster Abbey. This symbol was believed to be the pillow on which Jacob slept, when he had his vision of angels ascending and descending a ladder to Heaven.[45] It was held in immense reverence by all Scots, and its removal was intended to drive home the fact that their country was now subordinate to England.

At Edinburgh Edward removed the Holy Rood, placed there by St Margaret, mother of David I,[46] as well as the Scottish regalia and an immense quantity of official documentation.[47] All were taken to England; the papers were never seen again.

At a parliament held at Berwick on 28 August 1296, every landholder in Scotland from Caithness to Galloway was ordered to appear with signed and sealed evidence of his loyalty. This list of nearly 2,000 names, which included the whole of the Scottish clergy, was termed 'the Ragman Roll'.[48] The name of Sir Malcolm Wallace of Elderslie does not appear on it. Two names which do are those of Robert Bruce and his son. By reaffirming their allegiance to England, their Annandale lands were taken back from Comyn and returned to them.[49]

It is said that Bruce, who had given his support to the campaign in the hope that his own claim to the throne would be successful, voiced his ambitions to Edward. The King – with smiling venom, heavy irony or impatience; it would be interesting to know which – replied, 'Do you think we have nothing to do but win kingdoms for you?'[50]

Before leaving a country he believed crushed, on 17

September 1296 Edward appointed three key English officials to govern in his name. These were John de Warenne, Earl of Surrey, then ailing and in his seventies, Governor; William Ormsby, Chief Justice; and Hugh de Cressingham, Treasurer, soon to be the most hated man in Scotland. He was despised even by the English nobles for being a bastard as well as a political upstart,[51] and suspected of appropriating dues intended for the rebuilding of Berwick to his own use.[52]

Another observation credited to Edward is one he made to Warenne on leaving Scotland, which well expressed his contempt for the country: 'He does good business who rids himself of dirt.'[53]

Had Edward appointed moderate Scottish nobles as viceroys, the country would likely have come to accept in time the changed order of things. His action in ramming home his own power over what he believed to be a defeated people aroused in them a determination to rise and fight.

For the remaining ten years of his life, Edward was to make repeated attempts to conquer Scotland, without ever succeeding, and he died 'valiant and determined as ever, but a broken man'.[54]

Winter was now approaching, a time when it was impossible to continue hostilities. Shelter for a vast number of men could not be found. Forage for horses was quickly exhausted. Stores could be held up for weeks if the weather was severe.

If Edward, snug in his palace, imagined all was quiet north of the Borders, he was soon to be sharply disillusioned. A certain conspirator in Glasgow was already busily at work, and at the same time, in John of Fordun's striking phrase, 'William Wallace lifted up his head.'[55]

7 Wallace Opens the Attack

Chief of Brigands in Scotland.
Hemingburgh

The most influential churchman in Scotland was William Fraser, the Bishop of St Andrews, an old man who was so Norman that he could readily be described as pro-English.

Men looked, therefore, to the next in importance for some sort of leadership. This was Robert Wishart, the Bishop of Glasgow, who had been one of the regents following the Maid of Norway's death. Although this office had ended on Balliol's accession, Wishart continued to support King John as the legally appointed ruler of Scotland.

The Church in Scotland was intensely jealous of its rights and liberties. Edward's effort to anglicize it had merely stiffened its determination to throw off the English influence that had been forced on it. Whether or not he realized it, Edward had more reason to be wary of the resistance of the Church than that of the nobles.[1] The spirit of opposition may well have originated in the ecclesiastical hierarchy, but it required a man of Wallace's vigour to transform its plans into reality.

What is certain is that lines of communication stretched from the Bishop's palace in Glasgow to every diocese in the country, bringing him reports of displaced clergy and of a bitterly resentful people only waiting for an opportunity to strike back at their enemy. Among them would possibly be the wealthy incumbent of Kilspindie. The two men might have been of an age, and perhaps shared a friendship that ensured that the priest kept his superior informed of activities in his area. Wishart could certainly not have missed hearing of Wallace's activities so close to Glasgow. He would know that Sir Malcolm senior had been among those slain for refusing to add his name to the Ragman Roll.

It is believed that at one time Wallace was intended for the Church, an institution which could grant high honours to its favoured sons.[2] Two of his uncles were priests, and his father had been connected with Paisley Abbey.

The distance between Riccarton and Glasgow was small, and Wallace certainly travelled it at least once, and probably several times, to confer with Wishart. The bishop must have been struck at once by the young man's presence, and by his tall, strong, upright bearing. Churchman and outlaw must have discovered that marvellous chord of mutual trust and shared endeavour that transcends age and class.

If the Bishop could find others to raise the banner of rebellion elsewhere in Scotland, Wallace was his man in the south. Nevertheless, there was to be no question of mobilizing a disorganized rabble without aim or direction. If Scotland rose, it would do so to return to power her rightfully annointed king, the symbol of her independence from English rule. All must be done, then, in Balliol's name.

To this end, Wishart found a cautious supporter in James the Steward, one of the late Guardians of the kingdom. James Stewart owned vast estates in Renfrew, Lauderdale, Lothian and Bute and was a kinsman of Sir William Douglas, the defender of Berwick Castle. Douglas's courageous example in coming out for Wallace, and Wallace's own successes, persuaded Stewart to agree to ally himself with Wishart.[3]

Among the knights taken prisoner after the rout at Dunbar were young Andrew de Moray, his father, Sir Andrew, and an uncle known as 'le Riche' by virtue of his wealth.[4] He and Sir Andrew senior were imprisoned in the Tower, but young de Moray was sent to be held in Chester Castle.[5]

The family, which was Celtic, owned estates which included the lordship of Bothwell, an immense stretch of land in Lanarkshire. Strategically placed, Bothwell Castle was situated on the north bank of the River Clyde and was only one of the family's fortifications in Scotland. It changed hands frequently in the struggle for independence, and in 1296 was seized by Edward and strongly garrisoned.[6] Other of their lands and castles were in Moray, Banff, Inverness and Ross, such as Avoch, Peltry, Croy, Boharm, Brachlie, Arturlies and Arndilly.[7] The family was placed firmly on the nationalist side.

Many of those captured at Dunbar were, in accordance with the procedures of the time, offered their freedom if they would take arms for England in the planned invasion of Flanders. Among those who accepted were John Comyn 'the Red', son of the Earl of Buchan. Sir Andrew de Moray senior refused, but his brother, Sir William, chafing at his imprisonment, accepted.

Nevertheless, it indicates how wary Edward was of the de Morays as a threat to himself in northern Scotland. Sir Andrew was kept in the Tower, dying there before November 1300, while Sir William, although he served with Edward's forces, was refused permission to return home and kept under terms of considerable severity, dying in straitened circumstances at about the same time.[8]

The de Morays, too, had important connections with the Church. David de Moravia, the younger brother of Sir Andrew and Sir William, was a priest at Bothwell in 1296.[9] Following their imprisonment, he became head of the family and began to make such rapid progress in his profession that one may suspect the hidden influence of Robert Wishart. He was a canon at Elgin in 1297 or 1298 and became Bishop of Moray and Caithness in 1299.[10] Among his later achievements was the foundation of the Scots College in Paris in 1325.[11] It consisted of a charitable fund for the support and education at the University of Paris of four poor scholars from the diocese of Moray.

David de Moravia was as whole-hearted a patriot as his nephew, young Andrew de Moray, and vigorously supported Wishart's plans for a northern uprising. Unlike Wishart and Lamberton, who both returned at times to Edward's peace, David de Moravia steadfastly refused to give an oath of allegiance to England.[12] When Bruce made his bid for the throne in 1306, David was one of the first to rally supporters to his cause.[13]

The peculiar history of Moray has already been mentioned. Its people owed support direct to the monarch and not to a feudal superior. An insurrection, then, begun in Moray in support of King John Balliol, had an excellent chance of success.

Wishart had already earmarked one eager, passionately patriotic young man very nearly on his doorstep, who had gathered round him a number of like-minded companions. What was required was someone of a similar nature to Wallace in the Celtic north. Young de Moray must, in consequence, be fetched from his prison in Chester.

Such evidence as exists suggests he escaped at this remarkably convenient time through his own resourcefulness, although five other Scots with him were still prisoners there in September 1300.[14] It is, however, asking too much to accept that a lone prisoner eluded all his pursuers, until he appeared in Moray the following May to raise the *Vexillum Moraviae* in a call to arms. With the River Dee only six miles to the west, once some gaoler's pocket was the heavier for the bishop's gold, de Moray could have been aboard a fishing-boat and making for a quiet stretch of coast to the north, where horses and friends awaited him.

Certainly he must have had help to get out of England, and just as surely been in contact with Wishart during his imprisonment. A turnkey who accepts a bribe for aiding a prisoner to escape is not one who will quibble at secretly delivering letters or conveying answers to an agent on the outside.

At any rate, Andrew was free. He must have stopped at Glasgow on his flight north long enough to confer with the bishop, but his next stop was Moray, and his father's castle at Avoch.[15]

In the south, Wallace was again on the attack.

Well provided with arms and equipment from Percy's baggage train, Wallace decided to launch his first assault on an English fortification.[16]

This was the peel tower of Gargunnock, five miles to the west of Stirling. It was a bold decision, for Stirling Castle was heavily garrisoned, and the moment the news of the attack reached the town, a vigorous pursuit was inevitable.

Wallace first sent two of his group to spy out the land. They returned to report that the drawbridge had been lowered and that a number of labourers engaged in building-work were passing freely in and out. So secure did the sentry feel that he was dozing at his post.

Wallace at once advanced with his group of sixty companions. Finding the peel door bolted with an iron bar, he wrenched it free of the stones to which it was affixed, and used his foot to drive it open. The commander of the garrison, Captain Thirlwall, stumbled out with his bemused men, and all twenty-two were killed in the ensuing fight. Wives and children found in the tower were allowed to leave unharmed, but a quantity of useful booty was carried off.[17] In all his exploits, Wallace invariably spared the women he took as prisoners, and set them free.

This lightning guerrilla attack, so carefully planned and successfully accomplished, set the countryside abuzz with excitement. Stirling has been likened to a brooch gathering north and south at its narrowest point, like the folds of a garment. It was, in consequence, of immense strategic importance, and its formidable castle, set high on a rock, commanded a panoramic view for miles. There was a single wooden bridge into the town from the north, and two fords, one at Cambuskenneth Abbey close by.

The River Forth at this point was wide and fast-moving when swollen by rain or melting snow from the mountains, and was a source of livelihood for local fishermen. There was a busy market cross, a lepers' hospital and a Dominican priory, and farmers from the surrounding district travelled to the town with their produce. The English garrison is known to have bought from them, a practice continued when the Scots retook the castle.

Within hours, itinerant traders and merchants left Stirling, their ears ringing with the latest exploit of William Wallace. This young man, about whom tales had been circulating for months, had now had the temerity to attack one of King Edward's newest fortifications. The news must have been carried gleefully from one town to the next. What is certain is that an alarmed report went off post-haste to England about the outrage.

Wallace meantime continued his rapid progress, leaving the authorities confused as to his direction and intentions. In fact, he crossed the Forth north of Gargunnock, where it was narrower, then the Teith, and made his way to Strathearn, the country south of Perth. Any English soldiers he encountered were killed without mercy.[18]

Crossing the River Earn, he set up camp in Methven Wood and with seven chosen companions went off to gather information. It was apparent at once that he lacked a sufficient force to take the important town of Perth, but he learned that Sir John Butler, son of Sir James Butler of Kinclaven, was second in command under Sir Gerard Heron. Sir James, who had been visiting Perth, was on the point of returning home with a richly laden convoy.

Kinclaven is on the north bank of the River Tay, north of its junction with the River Isla, in country Wallace knew well from his time at Dundee. Concealing himself and his companions in a thickly wooded hollow, he waited for Butler's train to come in sight.

The wholly unexpected attack threw the ninety-strong English horse into disarray. Wallace is credited with dispatching Butler, while two-thirds of the enemy were killed before the survivors could flee for the safety of the castle. The drawbridge was at once lowered to admit them, but Wallace was so close at their heels that there was no time to secure the gates before the Scots poured into the courtyard. In fierce fighting, they killed the remaining defenders with small loss to themselves. Lady Butler, her children and women attendants and two priests were spared, the castle thereafter being set on fire.[19]

The news was rapidly carried back to Sir Gerard Heron, who must have seethed to learn that his castle and garrison had been overthrown by a man branded an outlaw. Wallace and his men would not have been difficult to follow into Methven Wood, laden as they were with booty from the wagon train, and Heron was confident of overtaking them. Dividing his soldiers into six companies, he ordered five of them to surround the wood. The sixth, which was to make a direct attack, he placed under the command of Sir John Butler.[20]

Horses were, however, virtually useless in heavily forested terrain, and Wallace, anticipating Heron's reasoning, had chosen a strong position from which to defend himself. Three walls had been run up, consisting of fallen trees laid crosswise, leaving just one side open.

At this point, Wallace was to learn the importance of the archer in warfare. He had twenty bowmen, but none was particularly skilled. Wallace himself had a bow so large that he was the only man strong enough to draw it, but no more than fifteen arrows.[21] Once shot, the bow as a weapon was useless, and his seems not to have been used in any of his future exploits. Thereafter it is the two-handed sword which was to become associated with his name, and a fearsome weapon it must have been in close-combat fighting.[22]

Wallace was now struck by an English arrow under the left side of the chin, through a gap in his steel collar, causing a painful and debilitating wound.[23]

By afternoon, finding himself unable to close with the Scots, Heron sent to Sir William de Loraine at Gowrie for reinforcements. Sir William arrived with 300 men and a strong desire to exact revenge for the death of his uncle, Sir James Butler. Their combined strength forced Wallace to amend his plans for indefinite resistance. Abandoning his position, he and his Scots moved deeper into Methven Wood.

This, however, could provide only a temporary respite. If they were not to be trapped, they must fight their way out. In the next assault, a number of Scots were killed, although three times as many English soldiers fell in desperate fighting. Cutting their way through Heron's lines, they reached the River Tay, only to find themselves at a point at which the water was too deep to wade across.

Turning to meet the enemy, Wallace and his group fought their way back, but nine more Scots were lost, leaving him just fourteen exhausted men. This must have been when he made the decision to give the order to scatter,[24] in the hope that his companions could evade the English as darkness set in, for Wallace was on his own when he reached the ford on the River Earn, only to find Sir John Butler and a company of soldiers barring his way.

As Wallace came into the open, Sir John must have guessed that this blood-stained, dangerous-looking young man had been among his uncle's assailants and at once drew his sword. Wallace leapt to the attack, killed Butler, seized his horse and galloped off, hotly pursued by some of Heron's men. Fighting off those who overtook him and killing several, Wallace rode south-east. Fifteen miles on, near Blackford, his horse foundered and he continued his fight on foot. Possibly he crossed the desolate stretch of Sheriff Muir, scene of a battle 400 years later, during the 1715 Jacobite Rebellion, in which a Stuart prince, descendant of a daughter of Robert the Bruce, sought to win Scotland.[25]

By the time Wallace reached the Forth, he must have been in great pain and suffering from loss of blood. He may have hoped to reach Dunipace, where he could be assured of sanctuary, but his weakened condition put this out of the question. And between him and the safety of Tor Wood, a vast forest to the north of Stirling, were the deep waters of the River Forth.

There was nothing for it but to swim across, and this Wallace succeeded in doing.[26] But, once in the wood, he was in such exhaustion that he was forced to ask for shelter at a hut occupied by a widow and her three sons.

Wallace was always able to count on support among the great mass of ordinary people. It is likely he gave his name, or the widow recognized his build, or else guessed he had taken part in the Gargunnock attack, for she at once committed herself to helping him. Having tended his wound and found him food and dry clothing, she concealed him in a nearby thicket in case his pursuers were closing in. Her name has not come down to us but her courage and resourcefulness have. Two of her sons were set at first light to keep watch and give warning of an English approach, while the third made for Dunipace, with news of Wallace.[27]

His uncle responded at once, but by the time he arrived, Wallace's spirits and physical condition had recovered with all a young man's resilience. He turned down his uncle's plea to seek terms from the English authorities on a promise of keeping the peace, and firmly reiterated his intention to resist the occupation of his country at all costs.[28]

In the meantime, two of Wallace's men, Steven and Kerby, had caught up with him, overjoyed to learn he was alive and not, as rumour had it, drowned.[29] Possibly his pursuers, having reached the Forth and taken a look at its sullen grey coils, had convinced themselves that no one could swim it and survive.

Wallace, however, must have been anxious in case his whereabouts became known. He wanted no reprisals to be taken against the widow who had sheltered him, while his uncle must have been equally determined to move his nephew out of harm's way. The priest, therefore, made horses and equipment available for Wallace and his friends, and all three rode off to Dundaff Moor, a hilly part of Stirlingshire, where they decided to lie low for the time being.

The lord of Dundaff was Sir John the Graham. This elderly gentleman, who preferred a quiet life, must have been highly alarmed at the arrival of this young desperado, who was now carrying out his opposition to England well in the open.[30]

His son, however, also Sir John, was to become one of Wallace's most enthusiastic followers and remain so until his untimely death at the Battle of Falkirk. The young Sir John was all for raising fresh supporters at once in Clydesdale but Wallace urged patience. The authorities would still be in a state of alarm, and he had no wish to clash with them until he had entirely regained his strength.

No doubt the elder Sir John made no secret that Wallace's presence might endanger himself, for Wallace was soon on his way to Gilbank, home of his cousin, young Auchinleck, then aged nineteen.

There he stayed over the Christmas of 1296, but once the festivities were ended be got to work on raising not merely a fresh band of supporters but men enough to form an army. The episode at Methven Wood had taught him that, while small bands might be adequate for quick raids, the only way to deal with the enemy was by force of arms. Sixty men committed to the fight for freedom could do much; 600 could achieve infinitely more.

To that end, his friends were sent far and wide, with the assurance that he was not only alive and in good health but ready to accept both men and funds to equip them.[31] Before long, his numbers had grown into a useful fighting force, consisting of peasants, farmers, small lairds, craftsmen and burgesses, younger sons of knights, and men inspired by the prospect of uniting to strike a blow against England.[32]

With his four close companions, Kerby, Boyd, Adam Wallace and Auchinleck, Wallace left Gilbank as soon as the weather allowed and moved to Corheid in Annandale. There he was joined by Tom Halliday and Edmund Little, two more survivors from Methven, delighted to discover the rumours of his demise untrue.[33]

It was now Wallace's intention to attack the castle of Lochmaben, stronghold of Bruce, Earl of Carrick.[34] It was of great strategic importance, being on the main route between Carlisle and Glasgow, a useful halt for convoys from England, and the means of controlling the Western Marches. Until then, Wallace had made no attempt to launch a full-scale attack on anything as daunting as a fully garrisoned castle. He had neither siege-engines nor armoured cavalry at his command. What he did possess was resourcefulness and courage and an ability to inspire men with his enthusiasm.

Leaving all but Halliday, Little and Kerby waiting in woods close to Lochmaben, Wallace took the opportunity first to attend mass. While he was doing so, Percy's nephew, Clifford, arrived at the church with several bully-boy companions. No doubt they considered it a great joke to cut off the tails of the strangers' horses.[35] Wallace and his three friends, hearing the disturbance, dashed outside and put Clifford and several of his group to the sword.

Pursuit quickly followed, and their horses failing through loss of blood, Wallace reined in and sprang to the ground. So furious was his attack that fifteen men were killed and the English fell back, obviously deciding to wait for reinforcements to arrive.

The instant they did, they pressed forward to the attack, and in the ensuing fight Wallace killed Sir Hugh de Morland, a noted soldier, seized his horse and with Halliday rallied the others and forced the enemy to flee. Sir John de Graystock, the English commander, was enraged on hearing the news and determined to seize Wallace.[36]

For all Blind Harry's faults as a chronicler, there is more than a suggestion of truth in this event. Wallace and his closest friends were certainly riding good horses, for his uncle from Dunipace would have had the means to purchase the best. To see despised Scots owning mounts superior to their own must have riled Clifford's group. To mutilate the animals was the sort of malicious act they had probably indulged in before, on the horses of Scots unable to retaliate through fear of the consequences. This time, however, never guessing that the horses tethered at the church belonged to a different breed of men, their spitefulness brought swift consequences for which they were wholly unprepared.

Meanwhile, Graystock had organized his own pursuit and was making after Wallace. At Queensberry, with happy timing, Wallace was reinforced by Sir John the Graham and thirty men, and by Kirkpatrick of Torthorwald, who had come from Eskdale with twenty followers.[37] The strengthened party now charged the enemy and scattered them, leaving, however, a strong group determined not to give way. Sir John the Graham had been on tenterhooks to demonstrate his fighting ability and leapt to obey Wallace's order to break them up, killing Graystock in the process.[38]

Halliday and John Watson, both with knowledge of the area, now galloped towards Lochmaben Castle, calling out to open the gates because the commander was at their heels. Recognizing Watson as a local man, the porter obeyed and was swiftly silenced. Wallace and his men ran into the courtyard, finding only women and children and a few elderly retainers.[39] So certain had Graystock been of success that he had taken his entire garrison with him.

Presently the survivors from the fight began to straggle in unsuspectingly and were at once put to the sword. Wallace's success was complete.

Before leaving, he appointed Johnstone captain of Lochmaben, the first castle he determined to hold against the English.[40] Kirkpatrick then returned to Eskdale Wood and Halliday to the Corhall district, no doubt under instructions from Wallace to harry the enemy in every way they could.

Wallace and Sir John the Graham, with forty men, continued into Lanark, where they captured Crawford Castle and left it in ruins, before moving on to Dundaff.[41]

Some time around 1296, Wallace had become attached to a young heiress named Marion Bradfute, or Braidfoot, who lived in Lanark.[42] She owned the estate of Lamington in her own right, her father, Sir Hugh, and her eldest brother having been killed by the Sheriff of Lanark, possibly for refusing to take an oath of allegiance to Edward.[43]

In some biographies she is described as Wallace's wife, and Mirren states that in 1296 she was pregnant. The Revd Charles Rogers, in *The Book of Wallace*, published in 1879, declares, however, that Wallace died unmarried and without issue.[44] Harry, on the other hand – and closer to the time in question – says they had a daughter who married 'a squire of Balliol's blood' named Shaw, and that ' ... right goodly men came of this lady young.'[45] Harry describes Marion as 'amiable and benign ... and wise, courteous and sweet ... Withal she was a maid of virtue rare.'[46]

Whatever their relationship, Wallace and Marion became sweethearts, but someone else had an eye on the wealthy girl.

This was Heselrig, the sheriff, who was anxious to effect a marriage between her and his son.[47] To achieve this, the favoured suitor must be got out of the way, and to this end several of the sheriff's cronies, including Sir Robert Thorn, forced a quarrel on him. Wallace, having just attended mass with Sir John the Graham and being unarmed, endeavoured to extricate himself from the threatened scuffle. With Sir John, he made rapidly towards Marion's house. Hastily admitted, the two men were let out by the back door and escaped through the maze of alleyways beyond to Cartland Crags.[48]

Meanwhile, Marion courageously parleyed for time to allow Wallace to get well away but eventually was obliged to admit the sheriff and his men. It is not known when she was killed, either then or some little time later,[49] but it is probable that Heselrig himself struck the fatal blow.[50]

Her house was put to the torch, either as a warning of the fate awaiting others who helped Wallace or in an attempt to conceal the deed. Marion had, after all, 'purchased the King's [Edward's] peace', and questions were bound to be asked by higher authority once the manner of her death became known.[51]

Wallace's feelings, on being brought the news, even at a time when the life of the individual counted for little, may be imagined. The grief and rage he had felt at his father's end was as nothing to what he experienced now. In some ways it marked a watershed, for it hardened his resolve to wage all-out war against the enemy. From then on, Harry relates that he never hesitated to stab an Englishman dead or cut his throat.[52]

In early May 1297 Heselrig considered it safe to return, and it is certain that Wallace was speedily apprised of it by sympathizers.

In twos and threes, so as not to attract attention, Wallace, Auchinleck and ten of his closest companions entered by various town gates just before nightfall. Advancing on the sheriff's home, Wallace smashed open the door with his foot and ran upstairs to Heselrig's bedroom, where he killed him, Auchinleck stabbing Thorn, his deputy to death. Heselrig's son, hastening dazedly to his father's aid, was dispatched as rapidly, then, in grim revenge, the house was set on fire.[53]

Reports of this latest attack on English authority were sent to Edward by fast messenger. He was, however, heavily involved in trying to raise capital to equip an army for

France and could give no mind to what was happening in Scotland.

Local disputes of this nature were of small moment. Let those on the spot deal with them. What Edward could not surmise was that the Lanark attack was the start of an armed uprising that would end only when Wallace had kept faith with his vision and driven every Englishman out of Scotland.

8 Irvine

A younger son, without rank or fortune or the experience of
age ... he betook himself to the fastnesses of his country,
resolute to right his wrongs in the only way open to him,
and filled with undying hatred for the tyrants of his native
land.

Murison

As though Heselrig's death had been the signal for which
they had been waiting, men came flocking to Wallace in
their hundreds. 'From that time,' says Fordun, 'there
gathered to him all who were of a bitter heart and were
weighed down beneath the burden of bondage under the
intolerable rule of English domination. And he became
their leader.'[1] Presently Wallace found himself at the head
of a fighting force of 3,000.[2]

From Kyle and Cunningham alone came a thousand
horse. Sir John the Graham, Auchinleck, Adam Wallace,
Sir John de Tynto and Robert Boyd brought their vassals.
One notable recruit was Gilbert de Grimsby, a Riccarton
man who had been King Edward's standard-bearer.[3]
Having refused to bear arms, he was chosen to carry the
battle flag of the leopards of England, yet despite this
honour he now abandoned the English side and joined
Wallace.

Two English chroniclers of the time declare that the
leaders of the uprising were the Bishop of Glasgow,
Andrew de Moray, James the Steward and Wallace.[4] The
Lanercost Chronicle goes further: the bishop ' ... ever
foremost in treason, conspired with the Steward of the
Kingdom, named James, for a new piece of insolence, yea,
for a new chapter of ruin. Not daring openly to break their
pledge to the King, they caused a certain bloody man,

William Wallace, who had formerly been a chief of brigands in Scotland, to revolt against the King, and assemble the people in his support.'[5]

It has been said that the outbreak of a revolt in May 1297 took the English by surprise, but this cannot have been so.[6] The fall of Lochmaben, the defeat of its garrison, Sir John Graystock's death and the destruction of Crawford Castle indicated all too plainly that what was under way was not the action of a handful of disorganized outlaws but a full-scale insurrection.

In fact, so alarmed were the authorities that they determined to stamp it out before it could go further. Although little evidence exists for the barbarity known as 'the Barns of Ayr', not only is it mentioned by Harry but it is recorded by Barber and Major and in the *Complaynt of Scotland*.[7]

A large number – 360, it is said – of leading Scots were summoned to attend an eyre (council) at Ayr on 18 June 1297. As each man entered, he was seized and hanged.[8] The intention had been to trap Wallace but, coming late and somehow being forewarned, he escaped his intended fate. Collecting together what men he could, he barricaded the doors and set the building on fire, killing all within.

A similar meeting had been arranged for Glasgow, and now with all speed Wallace made his way there to warn those about to attend. Antony Bek, the Bishop of Durham, was expected, and Wallace intended to capture him. Bek was certainly in Scotland about this time, but perhaps somewhat later than Harry suggests, for Edward sent him north to report on the attack at Scone.[9] Wallace and his men engaged the English and inflicted serious losses in retaliation for the Barns of Ayr, but Bek fled south and took refuge in Bothwell Castle, then in the hands of Sir Aymer de Valence.[10] Unable to draw him out, Wallace abandoned the fruitless exercise and returned to Glasgow, certainly to receive fresh instructions and encouragement from Wishart.

In the north, Andrew de Moray had raised the banner of freedom and was devastating every English-held fortification from Banff to Inverness.

This intense activity north of the Borders must have produced a stream of reports for England, with Edward finally becoming aware of a situation which was rapidly getting out of hand. But all his energies were channelled into his preparations for war in France, and it was not in his nature to abandon his plans once made.

In the meantime, certain Scottish lords captured at Dunbar had been offered their freedom to return home, provided they raise men and money for Edward's army.[11] They included John Comyn, Earl of Buchan, Comyn of Badenoch, Alexander de Balliol and the Earl of Menteith, and it is suggested they arrived in Scotland unaware that the country was in a state of armed insurrection.[12]

If Edward knew what was going on, so did the Comyns and their supporters, for one of the conditions for their release was that they deal with the uprising in the north, organized by Andrew de Moray, a Comyn kinsman.[13] The Scottish nobles would certainly have been kept informed of matters at home following Dunbar. Just as Wishart kept in touch with Wallace, he is likewise certain to have sounded out the Comyns during their enforced stay in England.

After two weeks in the saddle, the Scottish party would have been thankful of a break, and where better than at Glasgow? There Wishart would have apprised them of events in the north, but already, once the Comyns crossed the Borders, they would have learned about Wallace's achievements in the south. Lochmaben, for instance, was now in Scottish hands, and the whole of Galloway was in a state of increasing mobilization.

The Comyns faced another week before they would reach their northern lands, and it is likely they set off for them without delay.

Passing south of them went Wallace and his army, intent on a daring enterprise at Scone. To his ranks had come an important supporter, probably due to Wishart's influence. This was Sir William Douglas, the one-time governor of Berwick Castle, and his appearance on Wallace's side at once lent respectability to the activities of the people's army.[14]

Sir William Douglas was a man to be reckoned with. He

had carried off Eleanor de Ferrers, an English widow who had been visiting relations in Scotland, and forced her to marry him.[15] He was related to the Wallaces' feudal lord, James Stewart, his first wife having been the Steward's sister.

There is some question as to whether or not Douglas was involved in the affair at Scone, but on 12 June 1297 Edward confiscated his estates in Northumberland and Essex, which indicates he no longer regarded Douglas as loyal to himself.[16]

The choice of Scone for Wallace's attack had special significance. It was the place where Scotland's kings had been crowned, and the importance of the Celtic connection has already been noted.[17] Nor had Scotland forgotten the removal of the sacred Stone of Destiny by Edward the previous year, an act of such singular insensitivity that, perhaps more than any other, fuelled the deepest rage against England.

'The temper of Scotland at that season,' says Lord Hailes, 'required vigilance, courage, liberality and moderation in its rulers. The ministers of Edward displayed none of these qualities. While other objects of interest or ambition occupied his thoughts, the administration of his officers became more and more abhorred and feeble.'[18]

Six miles to the west of Scone was Kilspindie, and one may be certain that Wallace's uncle poured into his nephew's receptive ear a bitter recrimination of Edward's theft of the ancient symbol of Scottish independence.

Scone was the headquarters of the English Justiciar, William Ormsby. He was a bullying tyrant and detested by all Scots as he presided in judgment over those dilatory in making their oath of allegiance. When they finally and unwillingly did so, the clerks extracted a penny from each man, ' ... whereby they became wealthy fellows'.[19]

Wallace's attack took place in May 1297. He very nearly captured Ormsby. Forewarned, the Justiciar fled in time, but he abandoned a wealth of booty which fell to the Scots, who killed a number of the enemy.[20] Ormsby made for his Northumberland estates and presently received Edward's orders to raise troops in the north of England for an intended invasion of Scotland.[21]

Hemingburgh relates that Wallace and his men ' ... proceeded not now in secret as before, but openly, putting to the sword all the English they could find beyond the Scottish sea [River Forth], turning themselves afterwards to the siege of castles'.[22] In addition, according to the chroniclers, Wallace's fiercest hostility focused on English priests. They were driven without mercy from the country, any who resisted being killed.[23]

In August an appeal for aid arrived for Wallace from an old friend, Duncan of Lorn, who sent word that Campbell of Lochawe had been seized by MacFadyen, the English-appointed lord of Argyll and Lorn.

Wallace responded with alacrity, defeated MacFadyen's forces and re-established Campbell and Duncan in their ancestral lands. At Ardchattan, a large number rallied to Wallace's standard, including Sir John Ramsay of Auchterhouse, who had long held out against Edward's man, the Earl of Strathearn. Sir Alexander of Argyll then captured the Steward's castle of Glasrog and invaded the lands of another English liege, Alexander of the Isles. The uprising in Argyll and Ross, which comprised the entire west of Scotland from the Firth of Clyde to Loch Broom, was under way.

Meanwhile, in the east, Macduff, the Earl of Fife, had raised his clansmen and with his two sons gathered 'the gentlemen of Fife', who were to fight so bravely at the Battle of Falkirk.[24]

By 1 August, however, his uprising had failed, and Warenne reported from Berwick that Macduff and his sons had been captured by the Earl of Strathearn.[25] It is noticeable, however, that the earl, although holding back from allying himself with Wallace, made no attempt to send his captives to England.

On reaching the safety of his father's castle of Avoch, Andrew de Moray was joined by Alexander Pilche, a Flemish burgess of Inverness, a town strongly garrisoned by the English and an important shipbuilding centre.[26] On hearing that the entire province was rising, the remaining burgesses abandoned their allegiance to Edward and hastened to join de Moray.

In Aberdeen, the sheriff, Sir Henry de Lazom, seized control of the castle in support of de Moray, and the entire county rose in the name of King John Balliol.[27]

De Moray then led his army across country, attacking every fortification and harassing and killing its garrison.[28] His tactics were so similar to Wallace's that one might accept that the Bishop of Glasgow had informed him how successfully they had worked in the south. As soon as an English force advanced, the Scots broke off hostilities and retreated into the sort of wild country in which mounted men were unable to manœuvre.

Certainly among those pursuing him were the Comyns, but how industriously they did so may be open to question.[29] Professing themselves unable to close with de Moray's force, the Earl of Buchan and Alexander Comyn received fresh instructions from Edward, to remain in the north and deal with the uprising in Aberdeen.

In Canterbury, the King was now sufficiently alarmed by the reports reaching him to issue an order beginning: 'There are many persons who disturb the peace and quietness of our Kingdom and make divers meetings, conventicles, and conspiracies in very many parts of Scotland, both within our liberties and without, and perpetrate depredations, homicides, burnings, robberies, rapines, and other evils in divers manners ...'. Action was to be taken at once to curb them.[30]

The Earl of Mar reported on 25 July that on the 17th he and his troops had met de Moray on the Spey 'with a great band of rogues' who had positioned themselves in a stronghold of bog and wood 'where no horseman could be of service'.[31]

Wallace's tactics at Stirling Bridge would be to place his army on a rise above a stretch of boggy land, and it has been suggested that he did so on the recommendation of Andrew de Moray, whose father had been a skilled soldier.[32] Nevertheless, Wallace had many times employed the natural advantages of the terrain in which he found himself, and was by then an experienced guerrilla commander, with an imaginative grasp of what would work best in the circumstances. He knew from experience that armoured cavalry was at a serious disadvantage against lightly armed, quickly deployed troops, and particularly helpless on soft or marshy ground.

De Moray now laid siege to one of the most important strongholds in the north, Urquhart Castle, and laid waste the lands of Sir Reginald le Cheyne, Edward's guardian of Moray.[33] Le Cheyne himself was captured, probably at the fall of Inverness Castle.

Sir Henry de Lazom, the Sheriff of Aberdeen, was now ordered to use every means available to lay hold of 'the armed bands of malefactors and marauders' who were devastating the country, but Lazom had gone over to de Moray.[34] Warenne reported to Edward on 1 August 1297 that he had '... sent to take Sir Henry de Lazom'. The plan to do so obviously failed, for the sheriff's Lancaster estates were seized in retaliation, he being described as 'a rebel adherent of the Scots'.[35]

On 22 August Edward sailed at last for Flanders on the *Coq Edward*, and he would not return until 14 March 1298.[36]

It was obvious to the Comyns meantime that only Wallace and de Moray stood between Bruce, Earl of Carrick's claim to the throne and the reinstatement of Balliol. If this popular uprising succeeded, the real power in Scotland would remain with the Comyns. If it failed, Edward would tighten his hold on Scotland and possibly, in retaliation, reward Bruce with the crown.

Although Bruce had made an oath of allegiance to Edward, he too was aware of the significance of Wallace's army, for it marched under Balliol's banner and, therefore, the Comyn faction. A Scotland freed from English domination should have meant a renewed hope of gaining the Scottish throne for himself but would, in fact, merely reinstate his enemies.

It is suggested that Bruce could not accept an inferior position to a young man described as a landless squire,[37] but the real sticking-point for Bruce was Wallace's adherence to Balliol.

Before he could take sides, one way or the other,

however, the attack on Scone took place. Edward apparently suspected Bruce of having a hand in the general unrest, for he was summoned by the Bishop of Carlisle and made to swear loyalty to Edward on the Bible and the sword of Thomas à Becket.[38] He was then dispatched to show good faith by an attack on Sir William Douglas's lands. This he carried out successfully, seizing Douglas's wife and children and sending them to Annandale as his prisoners.

It is possible that Bruce undertook the attack by way of settling a personal score between himself and Douglas.[39] However, the opportunity to place himself on the side of those who fought for Scotland's freedom was lost in his greater desire for the crown.

The result of the raid was that Douglas abandoned Wallace and went over to Bruce, probably as the only means of freeing his family, and peace was made between the two men.[40]

Certainly Bruce now began to stir up trouble in Galloway on his own account, perhaps on the advice of Douglas or at the instigation of the Bishop of Glasgow. In Annandale he made an unsuccessful attempt to raise his father's vassals but could only gain the support of his own men from Carrick.[41] These at once began expelling English ecclesiastics in the area and killing those who resisted, an indication of the influence Wishart was exacting behind the scenes. Bruce's activities, however, petered out and came to nothing.[42]

Inspired by Wallace's successes and de Moray's continued resistance in the north, the Scottish nobles, at Wishart's urging, now determined to unite their forces and make an all-out attempt to end the occupation of their country. With Edward in France and his ineffectual son, the Prince of Wales, in charge of affairs, the chances of success must have looked excellent. News had arrived that an English army of 40,000 foot soldiers and 300 cavalry, under Sir Henry Percy and Sir Robert Clifford, was making its way through Annandale, and the nobles and their vassals hastened to gather at Irvine.

With Wallace's triumphs so recently achieved, a fighting

spirit ought to have welded the Scottish army into a force
to be reckoned with, but at this point all went wrong. The
same divided loyalties turned plans for attack into
squabbling among themselves.[43] Probably those in the
nationalist party demanded the right to direct the
approaching battle. Likely Bruce, with all a young man's
touchy pride, refuted their assumption of superiority. This
and that lord took sides, to such an extent that Sir Richard
de Lundy, who had never sworn allegiance to England,
abandoned the Scottish side in disgust and went over to
Percy.[44]

This same Sir Richard might well have lost Wallace the
Battle of Stirling Bridge had Cressingham, the English
commander, listened to his advice.

Meanwhile, Lundy undoubtedly brought word of the
wrangling, which must have greatly encouraged the
English commanders.

Like jungle animals, armies in the Middle Ages gave
each other an opportunity to back off before an
engagement. This now occurred, and on 7 July Percy and
Clifford accepted the Scots' surrender and received them
to Edward's peace.[45] In return for hostages, they were
given promises of life and personal liberty, and the
retention of their lands and estates. Bruce is said to have
been required to send his baby daughter, Marjory, to
England, but this condition seems not to have been
fulfilled.[46]

Sir William Douglas took the surrender badly. He
refused to provide hostages and as a result was
imprisoned in irons in Berwick Castle. On 12 October 1297
he was sent to the Tower, and he died there some time
before 20 January 1298,[47] leaving a young son of three who
was to become one of Bruce's most courageous followers
and live ' ... to exact a great vengeance for the wrongs he,
his father, and Scotland, had suffered.'[48]

Bruce, in later years, would rouse his followers to deeds
of valour, but at Irvine he was still a young man of
twenty-three, lacking Wallace's marvellous powers of
inspiration. Wallace had an inborn ability to take a
collection of disparate characters and form them into a
fighting force, with the same passionate convictions as his

own. Men fought of their own free will for his cause, not at the behest of a liege lord whose sympathies they reluctantly shared.

The only success at Irvine was, in fact, carried out by a group of Wallace's Scots, including a number of Glaswegians, who fell on the English baggage train and killed several hundred of the enemy, carrying off an immense booty while their superiors were cravenly negotiating for their estates, without striking a single blow in defence of their country.[49]

If Wallace held his head in his hands at this fiasco, he did so only briefly. His character was always one that demanded action, and too much was waiting to be done.

9   *Victory at Stirling*

A man of Fate, given to Scotland in the storms of the 13th
century.

Lord Rosebery

Having achieved victory so easily, Percy and Clifford
congratulated themselves and prepared to return home.
But at Roxburgh they came on 10,000 foot soldiers and 300
horses under the command of Cressingham. He was
poised to launch an attack on Wallace, then reported to be
in Selkirk Forest.[1]

The three commanders decided ultimately to wait until
Warenne, Earl of Surrey, arrived from England with his
army. Such was the extent of the forest that troops could
waste weeks searching for a foe who had perfected the art
of melting away in the face of a conventional attack.

Nevertheless, it was plain that the authorities were in a
state of considerable tension at an uprising that showed
no signs of subsiding. Cressingham, the Treasurer, who
had been trying to raise money for Edward's expedition,
had found himself unable to collect any taxes and wrote
plaintively to the King:

> Not a penny can be raised until my lord the Earl of
> Warenne shall enter into your land and compel the people
> by force and sentence of law ... By far the greater part of
> your counties in the realm of Scotland are still unprovided
> with keepers, as well by death, sieges or imprisonment,
> and some have given up their bailiwicks and others neither
> will nor dare return, and in some counties the Scots have
> established and placed bailiffs and ministers, so that no
> county is in proper order excepting Berwick and
> Roxburgh, and this only lately.[2]

Wallace is credited by Harry as having appointed local sheriffs and captains from Gamlispath to Urr Water, which seems to confirm the above.[3] Certainly Edward's hold on Scotland was being prised loose, to such a degree that no Englishman felt safe within its borders.

It was now apparent to Wishart that the two armies of Wallace and de Moray should amalgamate. De Moray, however, was enjoying such success that he showed no inclination to abandon a countryside in which he could operate successfully.

Wallace, on the other hand, had the advantage of not being hampered by the possession of great estates, and his response to Wishart's appeal was to gather his men and set off for the north. On the way, he carried out a briskly successful campaign which began with the siege of Perth.[4]

An ingenious ruse was effected to gain entrance to the well-guarded town. Sir John Ramsay had 'bestials', perhaps a form of covered ladder, made in the forest and floated down river. The Scots then tossed stones and earth into the ditches that surrounded the town so that the 'bestials' could reach the walls, and swarmed up them. Wallace, Ramsay and Sir John the Graham carried the onslaught into the castle and wiped out the English garrison. Ruthven, who had brought thirty men to Wallace's army, distinguished himself in the fighting and was rewarded by being appointed sheriff, with the hereditary lieutenancy of Strathearn.[5]

Wallace now turned east, to Cupar, where he found that the English abbot had fled on hearing of his approach. He then crossed the Tay and joined up with Bishop Sinclair at Glamis. Brechin was reached the same night. Next morning Wallace rode through Mearns to Dunottar Castle, with the banner of Scotland carried proudly at the head of his army.[6]

A large number of English had taken refuge at Dunottar, where there was already a sizeable garrison. All fell to Wallace's attack, the castle being burned and a church set on fire. The bishop is said to have pleaded for the enemy's lives, but with the Barns of Ayr and other cruelties inflicted on his people sharply fresh in Wallace's mind, he remained implacable.[7]

By 31 July 1297 Wallace was in Aberdeen, where he destroyed a quantity of English shipping.[8] Aberdeen was an important sea-port, used by the English to land provisions for their northern garrisons, and was the administrative centre for the county. According to Harry, Wallace then swept through the north to 'Crummade' – at one time assumed to be Cromarty on the west bank of the Moray Firth but now thought to be Crimond to the north of Peterhead[9] – and was back in Aberdeen on 31 July.

Cressingham, however, had received reports from his spies that Wallace was in Selkirk Forest on 23 July, and even with Wallace's genius for fast deployment, nine days is an impossibly short time for such a wealth of activity.[10] It is likely that he has ascribed Andrew de Moray's harrying of the English in Buchan to Wallace. Or perhaps Wallace dispatched part of his army westwards to back up de Moray's forces. Harry's account may be taken, therefore, as substantially correct.[11]

It would be interesting to have some word of the meeting that took place between the two young patriots who were doing more to achieve their country's freedom than all the great lords put together. De Moray came from a wealthy and privileged family; Wallace did not. Yet one can be certain their respective enthusiasms struck an echoing chord in each man's heart, without any of the sulks and bickering that had occurred so shamefully at Irvine among the barons.

In a short time, every castle in the north held by the English, including Elgin, Forres, Nairn and Lochindab, had fallen to them, including the important one of Inverness.[12] The loss of its construction of shipping for Edward's fleet was serious and can only have enraged the King.

Although details of the campaign waged by these two courageous and energetic young men are lacking, it is known that a number of nobles, encouraged by their success, now abandoned their allegiance to England and joined them.[13] Others, such as the Bishop of Aberdeen and the Earl of Mar, waited to see what would transpire,

although many of their vassals are said to have joined
Wallace and de Moray.[14]

By the end of August 1297, only the castles of Dundee
and Stirling beyond the Forth and Clyde were still in
English hands.[15]

Warenne's forces had now linked up with Cressingham
and Percy at Roxburgh, making a formidable army of a
thousand horse and 50,000 infantry, which included
veterans of France and Palestine, levies from Yorkshire
and Northumberland, and a company of Welsh.[16] One
should not place too much reliance, however, on
numbers.[17] Wallace is said to have had 180 horse and
40,000 foot soldiers, but it is unlikely he had anything like
that. A more realistic figure would be 10,000, made up of
men from Moray, Banff and Aberdeen, some from Fife and
Kincardine, and a large following from Stirling, Perth and
his own Riccarton.[18] De Moray had brought some 6,000,
including 150 armed cavalry. Lothian, as ever, stood aloof.

Wallace, meantime, was engaged in the siege of Dundee
Castle, the town itself having fallen to his attack.[19] Being
brought word, however, that Warenne's army was on the
move and making for Stirling, he delegated his lieutenant,
Alexander Scrymgeour, to take over and marched south
with Andrew de Moray.

It is likely that Wallace was in good heart and eager to
get to grips with the English, no matter in what daunting
strength they took the field. He had realized for some time
that a pitched battle was inevitable. The skills of his men
had been honed by their fighting in the northern and
western campaigns, and to melt away now into the
fastnesses of the Highlands, without engaging the enemy,
would merely repeat the débâcle of Irvine. Fight they
must, and with God's help they would win.

With him went Andrew de Moray, and to him is
sometimes given the accolade for the direction of the
battle.[20] But Wallace was that rarest of mortals, a natural
commander with an eye for choosing a position that
exposed the enemy's weaknesses, and with the flair and
imagination to employ methods of attack which a more
conventional leader would have dismissed.

In addition, Wallace knew the area around Stirling well. His uncle's church of Dunipace was connected with Cambuskenneth Abbey, close by Stirling, and he had forded the River Forth and ranged Tor Wood after the Methven attack. He had crossed and recrossed the Forth of his forays in the spring, and must have carried a clear picture in his mind of the terrain that lay between the town of Stirling and the wooded slopes to the north, known as Abbey Craig, with the Ochil Hills behind. And high on its rock was Stirling Castle, held since 8 September 1296 by its English constable, Sir Richard de Waldegrave, who was now about to lead his garrison out to join the English army.[21]

With the instinct of a military genius, Wallace now mustered his army on Abbey Craig, the land between it and Stirling level, with loops of the river from west to east glittering in the early autumn sunshine.[22] It was 10 September 1297. Warenne's army coming into view must have been a heart-stopping sight: a vast array of armoured knights, their armour glinting, plumed helmets, the neighing and agitation of horses, banners fluttering, the rattle and jingle of harness, men's voices, shouts and orders, all clearly audible to Wallace's forces.

In accordance with custom, negotiations now took place with a view to inducing the Scots to accept terms. Warenne, who was in poor health and anxious to reach a settlement, must impatiently have regarded Wallace's army of common men as little more than a rabble. He had earlier asked to be relieved of his command, but Edward had ordered him to remain for the time being.[23]

It came as an unpleasant jolt to him, therefore, when James Stewart and Earl Malcolm of the Lennox, who had undertaken matters on his behalf, returned with the news that Wallace refused to yield.[24] Two friars were then dispatched to invite Wallace and his men to come to the King's peace, with a promise of remission for past offences.[25]

'Take back for answer,' declared Wallace firmly, 'that we are not here to sue for peace, but are ready to fight for the freedom of our country. Let the English come on when they please.'[26]

This defiant message enraged Cressingham, who had been so confident of crushing the Scots that he had directed Percy to disband his army in the west.[27] He was an unpopular commander[28] and had come close to being stoned to death by his troops, possibly for appropriating their pay.[29]

Now he urged Warenne to attack at once, but Sir Richard de Lundy, who had changed sides at Irvine, warned of the folly of crossing the narrow wooden bridge that spanned the river.[30] Cavalry could advance across it only two abreast. Should the Scots attack at that point, a hopeless bottleneck would result, in which case, de Lundy pointed out grimly, 'We are dead men.'[31] He then offered to take a party of 500 infantry and mounted knights across one of the two fords, but the headstrong Cressingham would have none of it.[32] He may possibly have doubted de Lundy's fidelity, but at any rate the knight's advice was disregarded.

On the morning of 11 September 1297, Cressingham led the English van forward towards the bridge, watched in tense silence by the army of Scotland. It says much for the Scots' discipline and for the regard that Wallace's men had for him that none broke ranks – as had happened so often before, principally at Dunbar – to attack the increasingly tempting target that now presented itself as the English horse trickled onto the narrow track that lay between the two armies. On either side of this was an expanse of marshy ground, so incapable of providing a firm foothold for horses that the enemy was restricted to a dangerously slow progress.

At eleven o'clock the blast of a horn was heard from Abbey Craig, the signal for the Scots to fall on the English.[33] From its heights they poured towards the river, shouting, 'On them! On them!' as they were to do fifteen years later at the Battle of Bannockburn. A breakaway group seized and held the head of the bridge and so cut off the van from the rest of the English army. In rapid time, those who had already crossed were cut to pieces. Any who tried to escape floundered with their mounts in a morass of mud and were speared to death by the advancing Scots. Others were swept helplessly into the river and, armour-heavy, drowned in its chilly depths. Cressingham was unseated and killed outright in the mêlée, while men and horses screamed and shouted as they tried desperately to extricate themselves from the disaster.

Warenne turned his horse's head and fled from the battle-ground, pausing only long enough to appoint his kinsman, Sir William Fitz-Warin, the late constable of Urquhart Castle, governor of Stirling Castle in place of de Waldegrave, who had been killed.[34] Then, abandoning his army to its fate, he galloped south without stopping, until he reached the safety of England.

On the day after the battle, ironically, the Prince of Wales sent a dispatch to Warenne, ordering him to suppress the Scottish revolt without further ado. Such was the slowness of travel that news of the English defeat did not reach the Prince until fifteen days later.[35]

Desperate hand-to-hand fighting now took place, and the Scots, scenting victory, pressed home their attack ever more fiercely. Wounded and dying soldiers tumbled into the blood-riven waters of the Forth as the Scots took a terrible revenge for the atrocity of Berwick.

Among those who waited on the sidelines, until they saw how the battle went, were James Stewart and Earl Malcolm of the Lennox. Then, with an air of never having taken up arms with the English in the first place, they calmly led their men forward to the ranks of the Scots.[36]

Then the English broke and poured after Warenne, pursued by Wallace's troops cutting down stragglers as they ran and seizing abandoned baggage-animals and wagons.

Only one English knight of note escaped the massacre at the bridge.[37] Sir Marmaduke de Twenge bravely rallied a group of cavalry and charged through the fighting. He succeeded in reaching safety on the south banks of the river, but his nephew was fatally wounded, his body being borne back on a horse ridden by his squire.[38]

Of the 5,000 infantry and over a hundred cavalry who had crossed the bridge, almost all, including some 300 Welsh, were wiped out.

The moment Sir Marmaduke got across the bridge, the order was given to set it on fire, but the ford at Cambuskenneth was so close that the Scots, men and horses, ploughed through the river without stopping.[39]

As Cressingham's body was discovered, his skin was flayed from his body and distributed among the victors, a gesture of hatred unique in Scottish history of the time.'[40]

It is suggested that Wallace then followed the enemy through Tor Wood, Haddington and Dunbar and on to the Borders, but it is likely that his battle-exhausted men were urgently in need of rest and sustenance. There would have been little opportunity for sleep or food the previous night, when the armies stood within sight of each other. There were also Scots wounded to be seen to, tended possibly by the monks of Cambuskenneth or in hospitals in Stirling, and weapons, armour and riderless horses to be collected from the battlefield. A token force under Henry de Haliburton carried on the pursuit, which it did so successfully that the English garrison fled from Berwick, allowing the Scots to occupy the town.[41]

Among Wallace's immediate friends, Andrew de Moray was seriously wounded, an event that was to alter the course of Wallace's future.[42] Whether or not de Moray advised Wallace on tactics at Stirling, they were young men of similar outlook, enthusiasm and determination. In addition, de Moray's family connections lent Wallace's army a standing that, following the victory at Stirling Bridge, could well have ensured a firm commitment to his cause by others of the Scottish nobility.

It was Wallace's misfortune that he was to lose all those closest to him who had had an influence on his actions, thus depriving him of their support and advice: Sir Malcolm, his father, Marion Bradfute, Andrew de Moray and, presently, Sir John the Graham at Falkirk. The burden of leadership fell on his shoulders alone after Stirling Bridge, and while he accepted it willingly enough, the great lords continued to see him variously as a minor squire, an outlaw and a young man ultimately dangerous to the feudal grip they had on their vassals.

It is likely that the gallant young de Moray – described as 'one of the chivalric figures of Scottish history'[43] – was carried north to his family lands, to be with his recently married and pregnant wife, but he died soon after.[44] His loss was Scotland's, and he has never received his full share of the glory for his part in the struggle for freedom.

Eight months later his son was born posthumously, and he was raised in Moray until 1303, when Edward seized him during his invasion of that year and had him carried off to England.[45] Once again, this indicates how wary the King was of another Moray insurrection's focusing on the young heir as the hope of the province, and his intention to blunt the boy's nationalist feelings by having him brought up at the English Court. In this Edward failed, for young de Moray was to become one of Scotland's greatest patriots and regent of the country, dying in 1338 at the age of forty.[46] His sister, Christina, would marry Bruce as her third husband.

The Battle of Stirling Bridge, at which 5,000 of the enemy are said to have died, ended the myth that a battle would never be won without the use of armoured cavalry. It also demonstrated that an army of 'common men' was prepared to fight with courage of the highest kind in defence of their country's rights, and not as vassals in support of their liege lords. The victory wiped out the disgrace of Irvine and took a terrible revenge for Berwick, and as the English streamed desperately southwards, all Scotland looked towards Wallace as the man who must now direct his country's future.

10   *Guardian of Scotland*

Wondrously brave and bold, of goodly mien and boundless
liberality.

John of Fordun

Wallace remained at Stirling only long enough to
reorganize his army, before returning to the siege of
Dundee. Fordun describes him as 'displaying evidence of
a highly practical mind refusing to be deflected ... from
completing a task already begun'.[1] To leave a single
representative of English occupation in Scotland was
unthinkable to Wallace, but the news of the English defeat
had spread so rapidly that Dundee at once surrendered,
together with a considerable quantity of arms and other
stores.

More importantly, the garrison at Stirling offered to
surrender if granted their lives. In the castle was, among
others, the doughty Sir Marmaduke de Twenge, who,
with Fitz-Warin, was sent as prisoner to Dumbarton
Castle. On 7 April 1299 negotiations were agreed upon for
an exchange of prisoners who included Sir Marmaduke
and Fitz-Warin, but the latter died before the end of that
year.[2]

Except for the garrisons of Berwick and Roxburgh,
Dunbar and Edinburgh, many presently abandoning their
castles, not one English soldier remained in Scotland.[3]

Those Scottish leaders who supported Wallace now
held a council at Perth and elected him and de Moray
'Generals of the army of the Kingdom of Scotland' (*Gardein
du Réaume* or *Custos regni*) in the name of King John.[4] After
7 November, however, de Moray's name disappeared
from official documents, his hoped-for recovery having
failed to take place.

Patrick, Earl of Dunbar, declined to attend, which angered the council, and they were all for dealing harshly with him. Wallace, however, dissuaded them from precipitate action and instead sent a courteous invitation to the earl to join them. Patrick returned an insulting answer in which he referred to Wallace as a 'King of Kyle' – that is, a master thief. Kyle was, however, also the district where Wallace was born.[5] Wallace's temper fired up, and he rode at once to the attack, determined to exact justice for the slander. Defeating him in a hard fight near Dunbar, Wallace took the earl's castle, but Patrick escaped and fled to England.

About this time, Wallace is credited with the capture of Cupar in Fife, with the death of 200 of the enemy, and it is probable he engaged in various 'mopping-up' operations.[6]

It was now essential to give immediate consideration to the state of the country. The land to the south had been ravaged by the English, homesteads burned, livestock driven off to feed the army, and fields left unharvested or unplanted. Many Scots were on the point of starvation, and urgent measures needed to be taken if they were to survive. Foreign merchants had taken fright at the destruction of English shipping at Aberdeen and declined to risk bringing their goods to ports such as Berwick, occupied in turn by one marauding army after another.

The cities of the Hanseatic League, a group of German cities who had banded together for mutual commerce in 1241, carried on a lucrative trade with Scotland, and in 1829 a letter dated 11 October 1297, sent from Haddington, then one of the chief burghs in the country, was discovered in Lübeck's archives, which read:

> Andrew de Moray and William Wallace, Generals of the army of the realm of Scotland, and the community of the same realm, to the prudent and discreet men and well-beloved friends, the Mayors and Commons of Lübeck and Hamburg, greeting, and increase ever of sincere friendship ... We willingly engage ourselves to you, requesting that you will make it known among your merchants that they can have safe access to all the parts of the realm of Scotland with their merchandise; for the realm

of Scotland, thank God, has been recovered by war from the power of the English.[7]

Meanwhile, heartened by the Scottish victory, the Earl of Buchan, John Comyn, the Earl of Strathearn and other nobles abandoned their English allegiance, while during the winter of 1297 Bruce found himself on the receiving-end of a raid on Annandale. This was carried out by Sir Robert de Clifford with several thousand troops, who marched from Carlisle, burning several small towns and seizing some plunder. This action was apparently the mailed fist demonstrating Edward's dissatisfaction at Bruce's failure to send his daughter as a promised hostage after his surrender at Irvine.[8]

This foray having produced no noticeable effect on Bruce, a second raid was made in February 1298, the town of Annan being put to the torch.

Some little time after Stirling Bridge (it is not known exactly when) Wallace was knighted.[9] It was possibly done by the Earl of Carrick, for an uncle, Sir Richard Wallace, was married to a member of the Bruce family,[10] or by the Earl of Lennox.[11] Wallace had also stood as godfather to two children of the Earl of Menteith, so the ceremony may have been conducted by him.

On the other hand, it may have been undertaken by Comyn 'the Red', although his father was living under supervision in England, and he may have hesitated to endanger the lives of his children who were hostages in Edward's hands.[12] However, almost at once Comyn was to abandon his allegiance to England, whatever the consequences to his family.

The writer of the Cottonian manuscript states that the ceremony was carried out by 'a prominent man of the Scottish race' ('*de illa natione praecipuus*'), which implies an earl.[13] It seems unlikely that Bruce, who was presently to defy Wallace and his army at Carlisle, should honour a man who represented his enemies, the Comyns. In theory, a knight could grant another the accolade, but in practice it was normally carried out by kings, princes or earls.

Whether or not it was Bruce, Comyn or another who now honoured him, from then on he is described as

'William Wallace, Knight, Guardian of the Kingdom of Scotland and Commander of its armies in the name of the famous prince Lord John, by God's Grace, illustrious King of Scotland, by consent of the Community of that realm'.[14]

The decision was now made by Wallace to invade England, partly from a desire to demonstrate that Scotland had thrown off the chains of occupation but more practically to avail himself of rich stocks of grain and cattle in the northern counties. He probably invaded England on St Luke's Day, 18 October 1297.[15] The army was mustered on Roslin Moor and marched south. As it advanced, English settlers in Roxburgh and Berwick fled before them, only to find the Northumbrians themselves in flight.[16] The Scots fell to ravaging the rich county of Northumberland, cattle and foodstuffs of all kinds being sent back to Scotland's hungry population.

Then, moving east, they reached Carlisle and made a strong attempt to take its castle.[17] This was, however, held by the Earl of Carrick and his son, the young Bruce, who roused the citizens to defend their city.

Wallace quickly saw the disadvantages of being tied down to a lengthy siege on hostile territory and withdrew most of his men. The siege continued with a small force but was finally abandoned on 8 December.[18] Instead, the Scots turned to plundering the countryside 'for thirty leagues around', visited Englewood Forest and Allerdale 'with fire and sword' and got as far as Cockermouth beyond Bassenthwaite Lake.[19] Returning west, they made towards Durham and its riches, but in an unseasonably early start to winter the army was caught in a violent snowstorm at the intervention, so Hemingburgh says, of St Cuthbert, one of Edward's favourite miracle-workers.[20] Many Scots perished and the rest lost heart for continuing the hostilities. They might have been encouraged to remain had they known that Bek had fewer than a hundred horse and only some 3,000 foot soldiers at his command.[21]

The Scots accordingly fell back on Hexham, whose priory had been left in ruins eighteen months earlier by Comyn. Only three canons had been courageous enough to remain, and their dismay can be imagined at seeing the appearance of a fresh band of Scottish marauders. Bravely declaring there was nothing left to plunder, they defied the invaders before at last agreeing to hold a mass for Wallace and his men.

When the moment arrived for the elevation of the Host, Wallace went outside to remove his weapons, during which time the chalice, the napkins, the altar ornaments and even the missal were all spirited away by the Scots.[22] On his return, Wallace found the priests wringing their hands, and immediately ordered that the culprits be brought before him and beheaded. Needless to say, the articles were not produced, despite Wallace's threat. Several thousand men had been making free of the English countryside for weeks and considered everything movable fair game.

'They were not found,' says Hemingburgh drily, 'for the seeking was without intention of finding.'[23]

Nevertheless, Wallace took the priests under his personal protection, advising them to stay close to him at all times, for his men '… were full of mischief and little amenable either to law or to punishment'.[24] In addition, he granted two charters, one of protection and one of safe-conduct, to the prior and convent of Hexham.[25] After this, Hemingburgh, who frequently referred to Wallace as 'that brigand', appeared to alter his opinion and no longer wrote of him in such derogatory terms.[26]

The charter of protection begins: 'Andrew de Moray and William Wallace, Generals of the army of Scotland, in the name of the renowned Prince Lord John, by the grace of God, the illustrious King of Scotland, with the consent of the Community of the same realm, to all men of the said realm to whom the present writing shall come …'[27]

Although this makes it clear that he was acting in King John's name, it is doubtful if Balliol had authorized Wallace to do so.[28] Balliol had been moved temporarily into the Tower and was not the type of man to risk his neck by conspiring with others for his reinstatement. This is not to say, however, that Wishart had not been in contact with Balliol during his lightly supervised internment at Hertford. The bishop could well have advised him that a rebellion was about to be raised in his name, whether or not Toom Tabard dared to reply. Wallace, however, remained true to the concept that Balliol, as Scotland's crowned king, represented his country's independence, for which he was still continuing to fight.

At this time, Wallace had apparently not heard of de Moray's death.[29] There may have seemed no urgency to convey the news to him from the north of Scotland, particularly as he and his army were moving about Northumberland at will, and he would have learned of it only on his return.

Leaving Hexham, Wallace and his men marched north, meeting opposition from the garrisons at Newcastle and Durham but declining to besiege either castle with winter so imminent. At Ritton the inhabitants came out to catcall the invaders on the other side of the river, no doubt confident of their immunity. The Scots' response was to send a troop of lightly armed soldiers to swim across and set fire to the town. The survivors fled, crying, 'The Scots are coming!', spreading panic even further south.[30]

About Christmas, they recrossed the Border with immense spoil, having spent almost three months ravishing the three northern counties as they pleased.[31]

Wallace had now to decide on a new bishop of St Andrews. On the death of William Fraser in 1297, William Comyn, a brother of the Earl of Buchan and an adherent of Edward, was appointed to succeed to the most important bishopric in Scotland.[32] Wallace would have none of that and at once set out for St Andrews to revoke the decision.

Receiving warning of his intentions, Comyn took ship and fled by sea.[33] In his place Wallace elected William Lamberton, then the chancellor of Glasgow and a friend of Wishart. Lamberton was to prove himself one of Wallace's strongest supporters and would carry out a number of diplomatic missions to the Continent on his behalf. In June 1298 he was consecrated by the Pope in Rome, and in 1307 he was to be one of the three bishops present at the coronation of Bruce.

Wallace now directed his considerable energies into

revitalizing Scotland with new ideas. He is said to have made a strenuous effort to end the system of feudal vassalage, without which there was no prospect of solidly uniting its people.[34]

He divided the country into military districts in which muster-rolls were compiled, with the names of all men between sixteen and sixty capable of bearing arms. Over every four men he appointed a fifth, over every nine a tenth, over every nineteen a twentieth, and so on. To enforce the principle of conscription, a gibbet was erected in each parish. Barons were warned to expect imprisonment or confiscation of their lands if they refused to co-operate in releasing their vassals for the army.[35] Wallace is said to have gone north to deal with 'certain recalcitrants' who refused to carry out his orders, and to have hanged several who defied him.[36]

'Such of the magnates, moreover, as did not thankfully obey his commands, he took and browbeat, and handed over to custody until they should utterly submit to his good pleasure.'[37]

What energy on Wallace's part is expressed in these words! What impatience must have gripped him, to find the great lords laggard when so much still waited to be done! Before long, Wallace knew that Edward would be back in England, ready to set about raising a fresh army. If it was to be defeated and Scotland gain in strength sufficient to maintain her hard-won freedom, the country had to unite under one banner – Balliol's, with Wallace as his champion. Such pressure as he put on the barons would certainly have infuriated them. As Sir David Dalrymple puts it: 'His elevation wounded their pride; his great service reproached their inactivity in the public cause.'[38] Against all odds, Wallace and his people's army had triumphed, and there must have been jealous mutterings at the power he now held.

Whether he was able in the ten months he governed Scotland to carry out his intended measures is unknown, but they demonstrate clearly Wallace's determination to end feudalism. His proposals must have intensely alarmed the nobles, with their implied threat of taking power from them and giving it to the people. In a feudal society, all played their part. Remove it, and farms whose produce kept a great lord's mansion provided with food would no longer be worked for his benefit, nor would he be able to maintain his standard of living if rents were withheld. Common men would demand the right to own their own land and decline to leave it to fight, unless ordered by the ruling authority of the whole country.

Nevertheless, an indication of Wallace's support among the nobles is shown by the fact that, in January 1298 and again in May of the same year, when summoned to an English parliament at York, not one Scottish baron turned up.[39] Sir Gartenet of Mar, Sir Alexander Comyn and Sir Reginald le Cheyne all abandoned their allegiance to England. John Comyn 'the Red' now came out in favour of Wallace and was to continue hostilities against the English until his capitulation in 1304.

In the spring of 1298 Wallace was still busy with internal reorganization. On 29 March he granted the hereditary constableship of Dundee to Alexander Scrymgeour, 'for his faithful service and aid in bearing the Royal Banner in the army of Scotland'.[40] On 5 December 1303 Bruce confirmed this gift, which may indicate his sympathies for Wallace. More, he referred to the donor as 'the Lord William Wallace', the term usually given to a landowner, which Wallace was not. The words were generous, for at the time Wallace's fortunes were at their lowest.

Spies would have kept Wallace informed of what was happening in England, and with the knowledge that an English army was being mustered for a fresh invasion, he would have seen as urgent the need to organize his forces.

He certainly devoted time to improving the military discipline of the Scots army. His infantry at Falkirk was well drilled and bravely withstood continuous onslaughts by enemy cavalry, unlike those battles when the vassals of the barons had broken ranks and thrown away their chance of victory.[41] Wallace must have been all too well aware, however, that he lacked the professional fighting-power the great lords could have made available to him, were they only willing to abandon selfish considerations.

The same hostility that existed between the Comyns

and Bruce and their supporters, and the same disparity of aims and ambitions that kept them on opposite sides, hampered all his efforts to give Scotland a secure and lasting freedom.

There was, however, no turning back now. Before winter set in, he would once again take on the might of England and – God willing – defeat it.

11 Falkirk

If you were to judge as I do, you would not readily place
your neck under a foreign yoke.

Wallace

Edward was still in Flanders, busily issuing a stream of
directives. On 24 September the northern barons were
ordered to join Warenne at York. On 23 October Ormsby
was instructed to raise a levy of 35,000 men. On 26
October arrangements were made for provisions of all
kinds to be sent from a number of eastern ports to Holy
Island or Newcastle. On 10 December he ordered that
levies be raised in Wales and report at Durham or
Newcastle by 28 January 1298. On the same day, Warenne
was named supreme commander.[1]

Most of the army had arrived at York by 20 January,
consisting of 2,000 armed horse, 12,000 unarmed horse
and more than 100,000 foot soldiers.[2] Included among
them was a contingent of Welsh archers.

Warenne at once marched on Roxburgh and Berwick,
retaking both, the Scots having melted away without
attempting to hold out against such a formidable force.
But, as he prepared to continue into Scotland, a dispatch
arrived from Edward, bearing the news that he had made
peace with King Philip of France. Warenne, in consequence, was to remain at Berwick until Edward himself
arrived. The army was disbanded, a token force of 1,500
armed horse and a contingent of 20,000 from Wales and
the more distant parts of England remaining with him
through the winter.[3]

On 14 March Edward landed at Sandwich and named
York as his new administration centre, the exchequer and
Bench being transferred north.[4] He remained there until

Christmas 1304. Fresh orders were issued as to the provisioning of his army, Carlisle being the mustering-point for supplies from Ireland.[5]

On 27 May Edward ordered his sheriffs to have their men at Roxburgh by 23 June, and next day appointed Patrick, Earl of Dunbar, the new captain of Berwick Castle. The English army now consisted of 3,000 armed horse, of whom about half were subsidized by the Crown, and 80,000 foot, including a number of Irish. There were also 10,500 paid Welsh archers, bearing a weapon which had hitherto not been greatly employed in medieval warfare, where close-contact fighting was the custom.[6] This was the longbow, of which the Welsh were soon to be considered supreme masters.

In an attempt to cut off aid for Wallace from the north and divide the country, Sir Aymer de Valence and Sir John Siward sailed directly from France and landed in Fife. On 12 June 1298 Wallace met them in the Forest of Blackearnside and inflicted a severe defeat. Sir John the Graham was said to have been wounded in the encounter, and so may not have been completely fit a month later at Falkirk.[7] Harry gives a touching portrait of Wallace, in the blazing heat, carrying water from his helmet from a nearby brook to his wounded during a momentary lull in the battle.[8]

In early July the Scots attacked Roxburgh Castle, but it was heavily garrisoned and they suffered many casualties.

Meanwhile, Edward burned the abbeys of Melrose, Kelso and Dryburgh and reached Kirkliston, west of Edinburgh. There he discovered that his provision ships from Berwick had failed to arrive, having been delayed by contrary winds.[9] The countryside had been laid waste by Wallace's scorched-earth policy, and at once the English army suffered a severe shortage of food.

A Scottish force also laid siege, on 20 July 1298, to Carlisle Castle, which lasted two weeks, severely hampering the inflow of supplies from Ireland.[10]

From the castle of Dirleton and two others, perhaps Hailes, north of the Tyne, and Tantallon, between the Lammermoor Hills and the sea, the Scots also harried

Edward's supply trains coming overland, to such an extent that the Bishop of Durham was sent with a detachment of soldiers to seize them. His men, however, were in no better heart than the main army and were so hungry that they were reduced to scavenging peas and beans from the fields.[11] Bek sent back an appeal by messenger to Edward for fresh instructions.

'Go back,' said Edward drily, 'and tell the Bishop that in so far as he is a Bishop he is a good man, but that his goodness is out of place in this task.'[12]

Hemingburgh, the chronicler, had this story from one of the messengers, Sir John Fitz-Marmaduke, to whom Edward added: 'You are a cruel man, and I have several times rebuked you for being too cruel, and for the pleasure you take in the death of your enemies. But now go and exert all your frightfulness [tyrannidem], and I shall not even blame you, but praise you. And mind you do not see my face again until these three castles are burned.'[13]

Fitz-Marmaduke duly reported back to the bishop, and after two days' hard fighting Dirleton was overrun, but the other two fortifications were found abandoned. Three ships managed to land, probably at Dunbar, and for a time Edward's army was heartened.

The provisions included 200 casks of wine, of which only two went to the Welsh, many of whom were suffering from malnutrition, while others had died.[14] Having conquered Wales in 1283, Edward considered them a people inferior to the English and had denied them representation in Parliament.[15] He had no intention of wasting good wine on them, and certainly never realized that imminent victory awaited him due to these very same Welsh.

Those Welsh who got their hands on their niggardly ration of wine promptly got roaring drunk, picked quarrels with the English and killed eighteen priests who tried to calm them.[16] A party of English horse charged into the mêlée, and eighty Welshmen were killed. The remaining Welsh seethed among themselves to such an extent that the English believed they would desert to the Scots at the first opportunity.[17]

'Let them go if they please,' declared Edward grimly.

'With God's help I shall be revenged on both of them in one day.'[18]

The urgent need to provision both horses and men was now so acute that there seemed no alternative but to retreat. Preparations were put in hand, but early on 21 July 1298 a spy brought news that the Scots army was only eighteen miles away, near Falkirk.[19]

At once the order to leave was rescinded, and by evening Edward had reached Linlithgow, where his army camped for the night. There was no fodder for the animals, and every rider kept his horse tethered to himself as he slept.

Once more, that quality of good fortune, which never deserted Edward personally, surfaced again. His horse, restive at its lack of food, became untethered and trampled the King as he lay asleep.[20] Had Edward, who was no longer a young man, been seriously injured or killed in the incident, the invasion would have been abandoned and Wallace's future been very different from that which befell him.

There was at once an uproar, men crying that the King was dead, and there were shouts, directed at the Welsh, of treason. Although two of Edward's ribs had been broken, he at once courageously mounted and gave the order to advance, although it was still dark.[21] His action calmed what threatened to develop into a rout, and by first light the English were in sight of the Scots army, massed opposite them on rising ground.

There is some doubt as to the exact site of the battle,[22] more still that Wallace should ever have fought at all.[23] His critics point out that there was no need to engage Edward and his vastly superior forces. Wallace should have continued his policy of withdrawal until the English, through hunger, were forced to retreat, contenting himself instead with harrying the rearguard as it went.

In fact, as Burton pointed out, Wallace followed the same tactics which served Wellington so well at the Battle of Waterloo, and it was through no fault of either position or the courage of his army that Wallace lost.[24] He could not suspect that the deadly longbow was now to come into its own, in a forerunner of such victories as Crécy and Agincourt, where Englisth bowmen were to overwhelm the French during the Hundred Years War.[25]

Barron, on the other hand, declares that the tactics which lost the Battle of Falkirk were 'the direct antithesis of those which won Stirling'.[26] Yet one could not expect exactly the same natural advantages of Abbey Craig, nor the bonus for the Scots of foolhardy commanders such as Cressingham, nor a narrow wooden bridge which would take only a pair of riders abreast. Every battle is different and must be fought in the prevailing conditions. It is all too easy to criticize the commander of a battle that is lost.

All the information which Wallace had received pointed to an army plagued by food-shortages, starving animals, mutinous Welsh and vassals and nobles alike sullenly wishing themselves home. A demoralized army is one already half-defeated. If Wallace could inflict a second decisive defeat on the enemy, Edward might well come to terms with Scotland and peace follow.

To back off, on the other hand, would relegate his army, as well trained as he could make it and in eager mood, to a year of marking time. Virtually every castle was already in Scottish hands. The north of England had yielded all it could, and a second invasion there was pointless. Let Edward retreat and Wallace's army would drift away to their smallholdings, farms, estates and trades, and perhaps lose their incentive to rally next time in such numbers when he raised the call to arms.

Wallace, therefore, weighed the consequences and decided to take on the English. Although there was no easy means of escape at the rear,[27] he chose his position with a masterly disposition of his troops.[28] His front line was protected by marshland, as at Stirling Bridge, and fortified by stakes driven into firmer ground behind and entwined with ropes.[29] His infantry of pikemen he divided into four schiltrons, an early version of the British square which, as Burton says, has 'baffled and beaten back so many a brilliant army in later days'.[30]

In his *Battles of English History*, George Hereford points out that Wallace's schiltrons were an important advance in the art of war, and he calls Wallace 'a born soldier'.[31] In

1314, at the decisive Battle of Bannockburn, Bruce was to make use of schiltrons in exactly the same way as Wallace and position his army behind a stretch of boggy ground.

Nevertheless, Wallace was accustomed to the lightning thrusts that are the hallmark of the guerrilla fighter. A pitched battle against a superior force required tactics of a different order. While Wallace had certainly devoted time during the winter and spring to drilling his army, he could not match the enemy in armoured knights. Now he was up against a king who had seen action in Palestine and commanded tough veterans from his recent war in France, unlike Wallace's comparatively inexperienced troops, however brave and willing they might be.

Among Wallace's supporters were some distinguished names: Sir John Graham of Dundaff; Macduff, great-uncle of the Earl of Fife, whose revolt the previous year had ended in defeat; the Steward's brother, John, with a company of Border archers and men from Bute; Sir Nichol de Rutherford, with sixty followers; Sir Robert Boyd and Henry de Haliburton. In the rear, with some thousand cavalry, was John Comyn 'the Red'.[32]

Wallace's infantry included men from the Western Isles, Galloway and other parts of the west and south, but comparatively few from north of the Tay. A company from Fife was present, eager to avenge their kinsmen slaughtered at Berwick.[33] Between each schiltron, Wallace stationed his archers under Sir John Stewart of Bonkill.[34]

As the English came into sight, Wallace addressed his troops. 'I have brought you to the ring,' he declared. 'Dance the best you can!'[35]

His confidence certainly inspired his men, for despite the massed ranks of horse and men facing them, with banners that included the Plantagenet leopards of England, all designed to throw terror into Edward's foes, the Scots braced themselves and held firm.

Edward then divided his cavalry into two main divisions.[36] The first was under Warenne, the Earl Marshal, the Earls of Norfolk and Hereford and the Earl of Lincoln. The second was under Antony Bek, the Bishop of Durham, and Sir Ralph Basset of Drayton. The remainder was under Edward himself, who now gave the order for the Welsh to advance. They refused and stood glowering and mutinous with their longbows, waiting to see how the battle went before joining whichever side looked like winning.

Edward, who must have been in considerable pain and suffering from shock after his accident, had no recourse but to signal Warenne's division to attack. The Earl Marshal's cavalry charged forward and found itself floundering in marshy ground. It extricated itself with difficulty, then wheeled off to the right in an attempt to attack from the rear.

The Bishop of Durham then led his division towards the east side of the marsh and prepared to attack the left flank. The schiltrons stood firm as the front line plunged its lances into the bellies of the English horse, inflicting fearful losses and soon being surrounded by dead and dying animals. But Bek's armoured knights charged with such fury that the palisade of stakes was smashed aside, and the Scots infantry found itself battered relentlessly by wave upon wave of cavalry.

Sir John Stewart was killed after dismounting from his wounded horse, and his bowmen were wiped out. Sir John the Graham, Macduff and his two sons and the gentlemen of Fife died where they stood.[37]

The Bishop of Durham now charged downhill with his division, and the Welsh, certain the Scots were about to be defeated, unleashed a hail of arrows from their longbows in such numbers that the dead on Wallace's side were 'like snow in winter'. A huge body of English infantry managed to smash the front line of the schiltrons, and the cavalry thrust forward into every gap as it appeared. The Scots defence faltered and was finally overwhelmed by sheer weight of numbers.

Now was the time for Comyn and his mounted knights to attack but, taking one look at the English charge, unbelievably the Scots turned and galloped from the field.[38] Their action turned the scales from what might have been a victory into a defeat so horrendous that ... 'the living could not bury the dead.'

The Scots broke and fled, pausing only long enough to burn the town and castle of Stirling.[39] Edward let them go, his exhausted and starving army being in no condition to pursue them far. Some mounted knights followed as far as Falkirk, including Sir Brian de Jay, master of the English Templars, who overtook Wallace in Callendar Wood. His horse became trapped in marshy ground, and de Jay was killed, possibly by Wallace himself. The only other knight of consequences who fell on the English side was, interestingly enough, the master of the Scottish Templars.[40]

After the battle came the recriminations. All the chroniclers of the time agree that, had the Scots cavalry remained firm and protected the schiltrons, the battle might well have gone the other way.

Various reasons have been given for such a pusillanimous desertion, without a single blow's being struck against the enemy. It has been suggested that, when the cavalry broke, Comyn's horse was swept away with the rest or that he pursued them in an attempt to rally the riders. One would have expected that the Comyn banner, raised high and leading the way back to the battlefield, would have been sufficiently encouraging for some, at least, to halt their headlong flight and rejoin him. There was, after all, a limit to how far heavy cavalry could gallop before encountering the tidal waters of the River Cannon, in which many Scots drowned as they tried to swim across.[41] Yet no attempt was made by Comyn or any of his mounted knights to return to the fray.

Comyn was certainly not lacking in courage. He had fought bravely enough at Dunbar, and an accusation of his nerve breaking at sight of the English cavalry scarcely merits inspection.

A more sinister possibility which does deserve serious consideration is that he hoped Wallace would be killed in the fighting. With Wallace dead, the way would be left clear for Comyn to reach an accommodation with Edward. He would once again be required to fight in the King's army; he would have to surrender hostages as evidence of his loyalty; but little else more serious was likely to befall Scotland's premier baron. Edward was realist enough to know he needed men such as Comyn to govern the country in his name. To have Comyn beheaded as a traitor would simply leave the way clear for Bruce to stake a new claim to the throne, and for a fresh war to break out, designed to place the Scottish crown on Bruce's head.

Comyn had immense holdings of land, and it must have raised his hackles that Wallace was determined to end the feudal system and make his vassals free men. His envy of Wallace was undoubtedly 'intense and bitter'.[42] It could not have sat well with him to find that all the adulation went to one who had no ambitions for himself, neither honours nor possessions. Wallace's army of commoners fought for the cause of their country's freedom, not because they owed allegiance to a superior. It must have galled Comyn's proud and élitist nature to find himself in a position inferior to a young man who had the fervent backing of thousands like him, all sharing his passionate desire to shake off English domination.

Let Wallace win at Falkirk, and the English would be forced to abandon their hold on Scotland, at least for the foreseeable future. Although Balliol was his kinsman, Comyn may have guessed that Toom Tabard was reluctant to return as Scotland's ruler. If he refused, Wallace would continue as Guardian until such time as the question of kingship was resolved. There was no certainty that Comyn would be chosen, for Bruce had the prior claim in law. Let Bruce approach Wallace with an offer of support, and Comyn could see his deadliest enemy become king.

Edward was now, in current terms, an old man in indifferent health. During the battle, the King took no part in the actual fighting. Although Comyn knew nothing of Edward's mishap, the chances must have looked good to him that the King's days were numbered. His heir was a very different personality, fond of pleasures, addicted to male favourites, such as Piers Gaveston, and lacking his father's steely determination of character. The Prince of Wales was a man likely to be amenable to persuasion. Make me king, Comyn would say, and Scotland will virtually be yours.

Thus all had depended on the outcome of the battle, in which Wallace suffered a disastrous defeat that was to alter the entire course of his life.

12 *After Falkirk*

He was deemed base-born by the Earls and the nobles.

Hemingburgh

The Scots chroniclers are unanimous in bringing a charge of treachery against Comyn but, even more interestingly, they accuse Bruce of joining Bek at the rear of the schiltrons when the Bishop of Durham attacked the left flank.[1] It says much for the doubtful popularity of Bruce at this time that such a calumny should be expressed, and the suspicion with which he was regarded as being one of Edward's men. Very likely it was remembered that he had defended Carlisle against the Scots' attempt to take the castle, and quite forgotten that in so doing he was fighting not Wallace but what he represented. Had Bruce ceded the castle then, he would have been allying himself to those who demanded Balliol's return, and thus given a clear indication that he had abandoned his own claims to the throne.

Bruce was in fact not at Falkirk but in Galloway.[2] At no time, then or later, did he ever take the field in Wallace's army, or consider himself Wallace's ally. One thing only motivated Bruce, and that was the Scottish crown. All his energies were devoted to that end. Had he put aside his ambitions and joined Wallace at Falkirk, the battle might have ended in victory for the Scots, but, to him, Comyn was one obstacle to his becoming King. Wallace, in quite a different way, was another.

Fordun says that in 1296 Edward retained Bruce's loyalty by promising the crown to the Competitor once Balliol was deposed.[3] As long as there was a chance of Edward's keeping his word to the Competitor's grandson, Bruce must have considered it foolhardy openly to oppose

Edward. In 1297 Bruce was just twenty-three years of age, as ardent in his way as Wallace but prone to the errors and mistaken loyalties of youth. Yet in one respect he never wavered: to win Scotland to himself.

An indication, however, that Edward considered him to have broken his allegiance is shown in that on 24 June 1298, a month before Falkirk, an order was given for £650 worth of Bruce's goods and chattels in Essex to be seized and sold.[4] Bruce was certainly active at the time in Galloway. He had taken Ayr Castle and was possibly keeping an eye on ships from Ireland making for the Solway Firth.[5] It may have been his information that led to the Scots' siege of Carlisle, which so hampered the provisioning of Edward's army. But basically Bruce played a lone hand at this time, unwilling to side with Comyn and thus Wallace and Balliol.

Edward had little to show for his victory at Falkirk other than an exhausted and starving army. For two weeks he remained in Stirling, recuperating from his injuries, the town so ruined and burned that the only building suitable for his stay was the Dominican priory.[6] Eventually he marched into Fife and devastated it, in retaliation for Macduff's stand, but he found St Andrews deserted and Perth already destroyed by Wallace.[7] He had Stirling Castle repaired and garrisoned with Northumberland soldiers, but it was now so isolated that six months later it had fallen to the Scots.

Unable to remain longer in Scotland through the deteriorating conditions of his army, Edward detoured home through Galloway with the intention of dealing with Bruce. Reaching Ayr on 26 July he found the castle burned and empty and spent barely three days there before continuing his retreat.[8] Bruce having followed Wallace's policy of destroying the countryside, there was no food to be found, and Bruce himself had withdrawn into the fastnesses of Annandale. Edward was determined to have something to show by way of revenge and burned Bruce's castle of Lochmaben before continuing on to Carlisle. There he remained until the end of the year. He spent Christmas near one of his favourite shrines, that of St John of Beverley.[9]

The King had little enough with which to congratulate himself. Wallace, Bruce and Comyn were still at large and all capable of rousing Scotland to continuing resistance. The south was nominally under English rule, but the entire country, with all its fortifications, north of the Forth and Clyde was solidly in Scottish hands.[10]

Nor had he left Scotland, as he had hoped, prostrate and beaten. So slight was the English hold on the north that, even as Edward made for York at the beginning of August, Sir John de Kingston, Constable of Edinburgh Castle, was writing urgently to the Lord Treasurer: 'The Earl of Buchan, the Bishop of St Andrews, and other great earls and lords, who were on the other side of the Scots water [the Forth] have come to this side. Today they are in Glasgow. They intend to go towards the Borders.'[11]

In the days following Falkirk, Wallace dropped from sight. He and his lieutenants would have made an attempt to round up whatever remained of his forces and see to the wounded, but to all intents and purposes his army was finished. The losses it had sustained made it impossible to consider further armed resistance without the help of the nobles, and they, Wallace knew, would never unite themselves behind a defeated leader when they had hung back from supporting a victorious one.

Sir John the Graham and Sir John Stewart were buried in the churchyard at Falkirk, and the scattered remnants of Wallace's army drifted back to their homes.

Wallace was, however, by no means alone. His brother, probably Sir Malcolm, the Earl of Atholl, a brother-in-law of Bruce, and others of his supporters still formed a close-knit band prepared to follow him wherever he led. It is likely he made for Selkirk Forest, an area which had provided him with shelter many times before, and presently resumed his guerrilla attacks on the English. The enemy's occupation south of the Antonine Line was exceedingly tenuous, and desperately needed convoys from England must have found themselves running the gauntlet of armed attacks by the Scots.

Certainly about this time John the Marshall, bailiff of the Earl of Lincoln in the barony of Renfrew, sent Edward an urgent appeal for aid. The Guardian of Scotland, with 300 armed knights and a large number of foot soldiers, had entered Cunningham and seized the King's newly elected bailiffs. Unless reinforcements were sent at once, they would be unable to recapture the barony.[12] Similar requests for help went off from Sweetheart Abbey and the abbey of Our Lady at Dundrennan, which demonstrates how inadequate the English occupation of Galloway was.

As though Falkirk had released their patriotism from its earlier hesitancy, the nobles found themselves uniting in a combined desire to resist Edward. With Wallace out of the way, the old feudal system revitalized itself. It was essential that the government of the country be put on a firm footing, and at Peebles, on 19 August, the Scottish lords met to elect new Guardians.[13]

Those who now came out for Scotland were the Earls of Buchan and Menteith, Sir Ingram de Umfraville, Sir David de Graham and Sir William de Balliol, barons who had stood on the sidelines and whose help at Falkirk could have been decisive. James the Steward, that on-again, off-again nationalist, like so many other Scottish nobles, took charge of affairs once more.[14]

Whether or not Wallace sent in his resignation immediately after Falkirk or some time later, he was not called to the council at Peebles, but as his brother, Sir Malcolm, did attend, he may have brought Wallace's resignation with him.

By then, Wallace had had time to consider his future and was making plans of his own. In this he had a powerful ally in William Lamberton, the Bishop of St Andrews. Lamberton had gone to Rome for his consecration in June 1298 and returned by way of France, where he endeavoured to persuade King Philip to aid his Scottish allies.[15]

On 6 April 1299 Philip sent an encouraging message to the Scots, but in July Edward made peace with him, which effectively ended any hope of French assistance.[16] This was augmented by a proposed marriage between Edward and Philip's half-sister, Margaret, which took place on 11 September 1299.

Hearing, on 8 July 1299, that Lamberton, the abbots of

Melrose and Jedburgh, Sir John de Soulis and other influential Scots were about to leave France, Edward issued safe-conducts to the captains of a number of vessels belonging to the Channel ports of Rye and Winchelsea to intercept them. All, however, evaded the English ships and reached Scotland safely.[17]

It is likely that Wallace and Lamberton met to discuss the situation on the latter's return, when Wallace reached the conclusion that Philip might yet be persuaded to help the Scots.[18] Who better to tackle the French King than himself? Where others had failed, he might be the one to succeed.

Wallace certainly sent word of his intention to sail for France to the Peebles assembly, for a quarrel arose over his decision to leave the country.[19] An English spy was present and sent an interesting account of the proceedings to Sir Robert Hastings. Those putting in an appearance included Bruce and Comyn, Sir John Comyn the younger, the Earl of Menteith, Lamberton and James the Steward.

Sir David de Graham, a member of the Balliol party, possibly at Comyn's nod (here was that damned outlaw once again taking matters into his own hands), demanded that Wallace's lands and goods be given to him, as Wallace was going abroad 'without leave'.[20] Sir Malcolm Wallace at once protested.

A violent altercation ensued, in which both men drew their daggers. The quarrel escalated and Comyn took Bruce by the throat, while the Earl of Buchan seized Lamberton.[21] The exact reasons for the flare-up of violence remain tantalizingly obscure, but it is possible that Bruce levelled an accusation of cowardice against Comyn over his desertion of Wallace at Falkirk, and Comyn's rage boiled over.

It is certainly evident that feelings ran high between Bruce and Comyn, the two opposing parties, but the need to put up a united front for the country's future was imperative, and the dispute was somehow patched up. Comyn of Badenoch, Comyn the younger and Sir John de Soulis were appointed joint Guardians, the latter presently being replaced by Bruce and Lamberton.

The new council wasted no time in opening hostilities.

Bruce returned to Galloway with Sir David de Brechin and attacked the English-held castles of Lochmaben and Annan.[22] Comyn went north, the Steward and his cousin, the Earl of Menteith, moved into Clydesdale, and Lamberton, de Umfraville and Sir Robert de Keith set about harrying English outposts in Selkirk Forest.[23]

In November 1299 Lamberton, Bruce and Comyn besieged Stirling Castle. So successfully had English supply lines been cut that the ninety-strong garrison were in desperate straits and reduced to eating their horses.[24] Wallace's suggestion of appealing to France had taken root, for the Scots now wrote to Edward, offering to grant the garrison their lives provided Philip would intervene on their behalf.[25]

Edward had scarcely reached England when he found trouble flaring up not only at his heels but among his own barons. He had issued orders on 18 September for 16,000 men to muster at Newcastle by 24 November, but had to abandon this due to the opposition of his barons. New orders were issued for 13 December 1299, to raise a force to relieve the siege of Stirling Castle.[26] His nobles proving no more amenable, Edward was forced to relinquish his plans.

In December Warenne made an effort to gather a force of 500 horse and 8,000 soldiers, but this enterprise too came to nothing. On 30 December the date was moved forward to 24 June 1300.[27]

In mid-July 1300 Edward, with an army of 6,000 and as determined as ever to subjugate his unruly neighbours, finally launched his campaign. Advancing from Carlisle, he retook both Lochmaben and Carlaverock Castles, before invading Galloway.[28] Reports from the time reveal that he was in a dark and brooding frame of mind. When the Bishop of Witherne came with two knights to negotiate for peace, he would have none of them, not even when they returned a second time at the Bridge of Dee to solicit his goodwill.

At Kirkcudbright, the Earl of Buchan and Sir John Comyn spent two days trying to thrash out a settlement acceptable to both sides.[29] Their terms were that Balliol be restored, that the succession be vested in Balliol's son Edward, and that Scots nobles have their confiscated lands returned to them. If no settlement could be reached, the Scots were prepared to give battle.

Edward, furious, refused to agree, although once again his army was in desperate straits from lack of supplies. Although sixty ships had sailed from the Cinque Ports a month earlier, with 1,500 men under Admiral Gervase Alard of Winchelsea, the provisions they landed were soon exhausted. The Welsh contingent deserted, followed by many of Edward's nobles, who had requested permission to leave and been turned down but gone anyway.[30]

In the ensuing fighting, the Scots were defeated and fled 'like hares before harriers', but not before a supposed Scottish deserter had led 200 of the English into an ambush, on the pretence of surprising his countrymen.[31] The Scots returned to harry the English, although Edward obstinately refused to abandon what was rapidly becoming a fiasco. At the end of August he was back in Sweetheart Abbey, near Carlaverock, his army disintegrating and his barons refusing to fight.

Finally, at the urging of his advisers, he accepted with ill grace the intervention of Philip of France. A truce was ratified at Dumfries on 30 October 1300, to run from Hallowmass to Whitsunday, 21 May 1301.[32]

Edward was also under pressure from Rome, where Lamberton had successfully pleaded Scotland's cause at his consecration the previous year.

On 27 June 1299 Pope Boniface VIII issued a Bull which declared that, as Scotland was a fief of Rome, he was its Lord Superior, on the grounds that the country had been Christianized through the relics of St Andrew. The English occupation would therefore end at once, and all castles and religious houses in Scotland be surrendered.

Even allowing for the time any journey took in the thirteenth century, the Bull did not reach Edward from the hands of the Archbishop of Canterbury until the end of August 1300.[33]

At a parliament held at Lincoln, on 12 February 1301 Edward's barons rejected the Pope's claim.[34] However, unwilling openly to defy the Pope, Edward requested experts in civil law at both Oxford and Cambridge to investigate his rights in the Scottish question. These delaying-tactics resulted in a document, dated 7 May 1301, asserting he had absolute title to the realm of Scotland, in property as well as possession. It was 'an extraordinary example of solemn diplomatic fooling, in reckless defiance and omission of essential facts'.[35]

Edward's further response was to issue orders on 12 May for a levy of 12,000 men, although he probably succeeded in raising only half that number, due to the opposition of his barons. Apart from light horsemen (hobelars) and mounted officers, all were on foot.

Young Prince Edward, now aged sixteen, was given command of his own forces under the Earl of Lincoln and sent across country to Carlisle.[36] Being brought to a halt at the River Cree, near Turnberry, and alarmed by reports of a strong force of Scots ahead, he retreated to Carlisle in early October, finally joining his father at Linlithgow on 30 December 1301. Prominent on the Scottish side which threatened him were the Earl of Buchan, Sir Ingram de Umfraville and Sir Alexander Abernethy, all supporters of Balliol and opponents of Bruce.[37]

There is a story that the Prince intended to visit St Ninian's shrine at Whithorn, but the saint's image was miraculously removed to New Abbey, near Dumfries, some hundred miles distant, and returned in the course of a single night.[38] One may imagine that, having learned from their spies of the Prince's wish, a band of determined Scots spirited away the holy relic to frustrate his plans.

Between 6 and 18 July Edward was in Berwick, 2 to 14 August at Peebles, 21 August to 4 September in Glasgow, 27 September to 27 October at Dunipace and Stirling, 1 November to 31 January 1302 in Linlithgow, where he had built a new castle. The winter was severe, and many horses perished. In the meantime, Philip negotiated a truce for the Scots to run from 26 January 1302 until the end of November.[39]

The Scots under Comyn kept out of Edward's reach,

and on 19 February 1302 the King recrossed into England, having achieved nothing beyond the taking of Bothwell Castle.[40]

On 7 September Sir John Soulis and Sir Ingram de Umfraville burned Lochmaben Castle and attacked the recently completed fortified tower. Scots losses were, however, heavy, and they broke off hostilities to move north into Nithsdale and Galloway. The countryside rose to support them, besieging Turnberry Castle and the rebuilt castle of Ayr.

On 3 October the Constable of Newcastle-on-Ayr sent an urgent dispatch to Edward, saying that the Scots were at Carrick with a force of 400, and requesting immediate help. Apparently that was not forthcoming, for in February the castle was still under siege and in such straits that the garrison ' ... could no ways go out with safety, and lost some in their long stay'.[41]

During 1302 Lamberton visited King Philip a second time but carried nothing of value, beyond encouraging messages, away with him. Edward had taken care regularly to renew his truce with France.

In the same year the Pope did an about-face and decided it was expedient to make peace with Edward by waiving his claims on Scotland. He had quarrelled with Philip and in retaliation advised the Scottish bishops to render obedience to Edward.[42] In Flanders, the Flemings had risen and captured a number of French fortifications. On 11 July 1302, at Courtrai, the French army was cut to pieces by the townspeople of Ghent and Bruges. With his country on the point of civil war, Philip hastened to make peace with Edward.

Several influential Scots, including the Earl of Buchan and James Stewart, met Philip in Paris and endeavoured to persuade him to remain their ally.[43] Scotland was, however, specifically excluded from the treaty signed by Philip and Edward and now found itself standing alone against the might of England.[44]

13   *The King's Enemy*

So long as a hundred of us shall remain alive, never will we
in any way be subjected to the dominion of the English.
                          Letter to Pope John XXII in 1320
                          by the barons of Scotland

In the meantime had begun perhaps the most intriguing
part of Wallace's life. He emerges from time to time,
engaged in guerrilla attacks on the English, in political
negotiation, in correspondence with Lamberton and other
important fellow Scots, in foreign travel. That he had been
crushed by his defeat at Falkirk and given up the struggle
for his country's freedom was very far from the truth. His
character and temperament were not disposed to an
abandonment of his ideals. If he felt any bitterness, it must
have been directed against Comyn for his conduct at
Falkirk, or against Bruce and other earls for having failed
to rally to the cause of freedom. What was done was now
past. Always there remained hope, and the possibility that
King Philip might listen sympathetically to his appeals.

Wallace is said to have sailed from Dundee with a
number of companions, variously described as eighteen or
fifty. According to Harry, some highly coloured episodes
then occurred that may be regarded, perhaps, as an
enjoyable fiction destined to glorify his hero.

Harry says that Wallace went twice to France, the first
visit occurring in April and lasting until the end of August
1299. Leaving James the Steward as his deputy and
unaware that his actions would alarm the Scots council,
who feared he might be captured, Wallace left Kirkcudbright with fifty men. The following morning their ship
was attacked by the *Red Rover*, a pirate vessel commanded
by a Frenchman named Thomas de Longueville.[1] Wallace

triumphed in the ensuing fight and not only granted de Longueville his life but obtained a pardon and knighthood for the pirate from King Philip. He eventually became lord of Kinfauns near Perth, where he married an heiress of the Charteris family.

Landing at La Rochelle, Wallace continued on to Paris, where he was welcomed by the French King.[2] Becoming bored with inactivity at the Court, he gathered some 900 Scots exiles and went off to fight the English at Guienne. On Guthrie's being sent to implore his help, Wallace returned to Scotland after an absence of four months.[3]

What is certain is that Wallace was so deeply involved with Scottish affairs following the Battle of Stirling Bridge that he had no opportunity, or even desire, to leave the country at that time.

According to Harry, Wallace's second visit took place soon after Falkirk, and so similar is this account that it is likely that the journeys are one and the same.

On this occasion Wallace left Dundee with eighteen companions and off the mouth of the Humber met an English pirate ship under the command of John de Lynn. Battening the ship's crew below decks, presumably because they wished to surrender, he and his friends boarded the vessel, killed its captain and wiped out 140 pirates. On Wallace's reaching France, Philip offered him the lordship of Guienne, which he declined. Nevertheless, proceeding there he captured 'Schenoun', possibly Chinon, and besieged Bordeaux. Finally, discovering there was as much intrigue in France as in Scotland, he went back to Paris, where he remained at Court for two years, finally returning home laden with royal gifts, to land north of the River Earn.[4]

There may be a grain of truth in this story, for pirates were active in the North Sea in pursuit of well-laden merchantmen from the Continent. John of Lynn may have borne down on Wallace's ship, discovered who was aboard and been delighted to let an enemy of Edward's go free. If so, Wallace's gift for influencing the unlikeliest of men stood him in good stead. On the other hand, if the story is fiction, it was designed to demonstrate Wallace's courage and his success against seemingly impossible odds.

Harry refers to Blair's part in the fight, based on an account inserted by Gray, who described himself as an eyewitness. Edward several times promised a reward to any sea captain intercepting important Scots sailing between France and Scotland. It is not unlikely that the King had a shrewd idea, or else received information from his spies, that Wallace would leave Scotland after Falkirk. A word conveyed in the right place may well have reached a pirate vessel operating off England, and the prospect of a rich reward tempted one to attack the ship carrying Wallace.

Sir Walter Scott included the story of the *Red Rover* in *The Fair Maid of Perth*, as 'given by an ancient and uniform tradition, which carries in it great indications of truth'.[5]

Some doubt has been raised as to whether Wallace actually went to France, but among documents found in his possession after his capture was one reading: 'Philip, by the Grace of God, King of the French, to my beloved and trusty agents appointed to the Court of Rome, greeting and love. We command you to request the Supreme Pontiff to hold our beloved William Wallace of Scotland, Knight, recommended to his favour in those matters of business that he has to despatch with him. Given at Pierreport on Monday after the Feast of All Saints.'[6]

It seems reasonably certain that Wallace was in Paris when given this letter. A further pointer is added in Bishop Stapleton's *Kalendar* of treasury documents, compiled about 1323.[7] One of the entries refers to 'certain letters of safe-conduct granted by Philip King of France, John King of Scotland, and Haco King of Norway, to William Wallace, enabling him to go to the realm of those Kings, to sojourn there, and to return; together with certain letters concerning "ordinances and confederations" written to the said William by certain magnates of Scotland'.[8] Frustratingly, the originals, personally handed to Edward by Sir John de Segrave at Kingston after Wallace's capture, have been entirely lost.

Harry writes that, when Wallace landed in France, he made for Amiens, where Philip ordered that he be detained and kept under observation. He then wrote to

Edward, offering him Wallace as a prisoner, but Edward, although grateful, declined.[9] This is so unlikely that it can fairly be dismissed. The one man who represented the spirit of Scottish resistance was Wallace, and Edward would have given a great deal to get his hands on him. More likely might be a suggestion that Edward asked Philip for Wallace's return, but the French King declined to hand him over. Philip could always use a company of fierce Scots under an experienced commander like Wallace to bolster the ranks of his own army.

Philip, in fact, welcomed Wallace, whose fame had preceded him by way of Lamberton, and made much of him.[10] It is likely too that this tall, good-looking, brave young man caught more than one feminine eye at Court, and it would have taken a chilly nature to resist their open admiration. One may entertain hopes that, after all Wallace had been through, such pretty girls made his months in France enjoyable.

But he was never likely to forget his reasons for being there, nor fail to try his persuasion on Philip. It was, however, now winter, when he could achieve little of value in his homeland. Stirling Castle had fallen in November, and the whole north of Scotland was firmly in Scottish hands. If he was to achieve anything more, it could be done only in Europe. But any diplomacy takes time, and Wallace was obliged to dally in Paris while argument and counter-argument swept back and forth among Philip's advisers.

At the same time, there were other Scots exiles in France, and Wallace, never one to sit idly about, may have mustered them to take part in the fighting in Gascony, as recorded by Harry. Mercenaries followed an accepted trade, making their services available to whichever government would pay them, and a man like Wallace, accustomed to command, would have found no difficulty in raising a company of soldiers of fortune.

Living under the supervision of the Vatican at Malmaison in Cambrai was the ex-King John of Scotland. Although no documentation of a meeting between him and Wallace exists, it is more than likely that both men met. Wallace had, after all, taken up arms in Balliol's name, and he must have been interested to see the man for whom he had dared so much.

Balliol probably agreed reluctantly to meet Wallace, for he would suspect that there was at least one English spy among his staff, reporting back to Edward everything he did. He must have feared being plucked from his comfortable estate and hustled back to the Tower, if he were suspected of collaboration with the man who had championed his cause.

It would be fascinating to know what Wallace thought of Balliol: whether he left convinced that his struggle was well worthwhile or if doubts began to surface of the deposed King's ability or desire to resume his reign. Even in a country freed from English domination, its ruler would require determination and courage to hold it against both internal and external troubles. Did Balliol appear to be that man? With his skill in assessing character, Wallace must have returned to Paris plagued by doubts, not as to the rightness of his cause but as to who was ultimately to govern Scotland if it succeeded.

With winter weather closing the roads into Italy and making sea voyages from one of the southern ports of France hazardous, Wallace likely waited until spring before considering his next move.

With events in Scotland being directed by Comyn and his followers, there was no point in returning home, for he could expect no help from the nobles. Accordingly he may have spent the year 1300 fighting in France with his company of Scots exiles, before another winter again set in and hostilities ceased.

There is no documentation that during 1301 he continued on to Rome but, given his character, there are strong reasons for supposing that he did. Wallace had not lost his passion for action against the English, and a direct approach to the Pope may have seemed the next logical step. There would have been little point in obtaining Philip's safe-conduct otherwise. By now, he must have accepted that the French King was unwilling to support Scotland in defiance of Edward and, as he had before, abandoned an enterprise that promised nothing of value.

In Rome, Wallace would at first have received a sympathetic hearing from the Pope, but in 1302 Boniface aligned himself with Edward, which ruled out any hope of assistance in that quarter. Whether or not Wallace thereafter travelled to Norway is unknown, but it is not impossible.[11] He had certainly obtained a safe-conduct to go there and would have been well received by the Norwegian King Haakon.

Orkney and Shetland were still in the possession of Norway, which also retained an interest in the Outer Hebrides. It was a long-shot that the Norwegians would be willing to raise ships or troops to aid Scotland, but Wallace was never one to dismiss a chance of striking a fresh blow against England. A long journey of this nature, undertaken partly by sea, could well explain his dropping out of sight during this time.

Nevertheless, he would have kept in touch with such men as the Bishop of St Andrews and David de Moravia, while friends and members of his family would have informed him of activities in Galloway.

At the beginning of 1302, Bruce was still one of the Guardians, with Sir John Comyn, but almost immediately, on 16 February, he deserted Scotland and went over to Edward.[12]

On the surface, it may seem an act of the darkest treachery, but there is some excuse for his behaviour. He had fallen in love with Elizabeth de Burgh, a godchild of Edward and daughter of the Earl of Ulster, one of Edward's most loyal supporters.[13] In order to marry Elizabeth, Bruce must come to Edward's peace or find himself without lands or possessions, an inevitable barrier to her father's assent.

One must not forget the influence a desirable young woman can have on the man who seeks to win her. Bruce accordingly took an oath of allegiance to Edward on 16 February 1302. His lands were returned to him, and the marriage followed.[14] Their union lasted until Elizabeth's death twenty-five years later, her love sustaining and supporting her husband in all the years of struggle which followed.

In 1303 Bruce was rewarded with the appointment of Sheriff of Lanark. In October 1302 he attended a parliament at Westminster and remained, outwardly at least, loyal to Edward until February 1306.

To modern eyes, how lightly these men of honour abandoned their allegiance either to Edward or to Scotland! Oaths were, however, regarded by the men who took them as little more than formalities and remained binding only as long as whoever received the oath was in a position to make it effective.[15] From the legal point of view, whoever broke his oath was regarded as a rebel, and his lands were forfeit. On his returning to the King's peace, his possessions were handed back. He might be sentenced to a short term of exile within a prescribed area, or to surrender his children as hostages. Edward, however, ever the realist, rarely treated his recalcitrant nobles with severity.

Every Scotsman of note, including the entire Scottish clergy, who were outlawed in January 1297 for breaking their fealty,[16] took the oath of loyalty to Edward during the War of Independence and broke it time and again – except one man. Wallace steadfastly refused to acknowledge Edward as his Lord Superior and went to his death as a proud upholder of his country's right of independence. The Bishops of St Andrews and Glasgow broke their oaths many times, and indeed believed it was their sacred and patriotic duty to do so.[17]

Resistance, meantime, was continuing in Scotland. In January 1303 Sir John de Segrave was sent by Edward on a foray into Stirling and Kirkintilloch, but he met with such fierce fighting that he was soon in difficulties. The Scots under Comyn had occupied a number of towns and castles and even invaded Segrave's own estates, and Edward was obliged to send Sir Ralph Fitz-William to aid him.

Now fighting alongside Comyn was Sir Simon Fraser of Oliver Castle. He had been taken captive at Dunbar but offered his freedom if he would agree to take part in the Flanders campaign of 1297. He distinguished himself with his courage and was rewarded with a destrier by Edward during the 1298 invasion of Scotland. In 1299 his Scottish estates were restored to him, and he was appointed Warden of Selkirk Forest.[18] But in 1301 he changed sides with such suddenness that he rode off on a horse belonging to a fellow knight. The disappearance of one's mount was a serious financial loss, and Edward himself replaced the knight's horse.[19] It is, however, an indication that Fraser had decided to join Comyn 'the Red' because the Scots were on the ascendant.

On 24 February 1303 Segrave found himself menaced by Comyn's army at Roslin, south of Edinburgh. His first division came under attack, and Segrave himself was seriously wounded and taken prisoner. His second division did little better, but the third repulsed the Scots and recaptured some prisoners.[20]

Rishanger states that Wallace took part in the battle.[21] Whether or not Wallace, remembering Comyn's betrayal at Falkirk, would willingly have taken arms in his forces must, however, be questionable. Yet, paradoxically, both men were still on the same nationalist side and fighting for the reinstatement of Balliol. But was Wallace, in fact, after his meeting with the ex-King in France, still wholeheartedly for Toom Tabard?

Wallace was certainly back in Scotland by this time. If he did indeed visit Norway, he would have returned home by way of one of the northern ports, for the country north of the Forth and Clyde was free of English occupation. He could then have renewed his acquaintance with David de Moravia, the Bishop of Moray, before travelling south to visit Lamberton. But there is the question whether, if he did come ashore close to the Comyn-held north, he and Comyn 'the Red' patched up their differences. With Bruce now in Edward's camp, Scottish independence rested solely on Comyn's shoulders. Did the two men meet and come to some arrangement about Wallace's future, perhaps at the instigation of his old friend the Bishop of St Andrews?

There was certainly no way Comyn, the great lord, would again defer to Wallace, but he might have backed a suggestion that Wallace go south and carry on a campaign of harassment against the English. In that way, Wallace with his followers could have found themselves involved at Roslin.

The news of his return to Selkirk Forest would speedily have attracted fresh recruits to his side, enabling him to carry out the type of guerrilla attack with which he had always done best. English garrisons in the remoter parts of the south must have dreaded to hear rumours that the victor of Stirling Bridge was in their area, and more than one convoy making the hazardous trip from the Borders been seized by Wallace's irregulars.

There are glimpses of his activities and influence behind such reports as that in some areas 'all the country was rising'; and elsewhere a castle had been attacked by four knights, 240 men-at-arms and 7,000 foot soldiers.[22] Scotland was by no means as pacified as Edward believed. Its spirit of resistance remained vigorously alive wherever Wallace's inspiration was felt.

14   *Wallace Under Pressure*

He kept alight the torch of Scottish freedom.
Murison

After the Battle of Falkirk, not one of Edward's subsequent invasions succeeded in doing much more than marking his progress from one town to another, watched by a people whose very impassivity must have told him he was no nearer subjecting them. He had the means of buying off the nobles through appointments, gifts of land or the remission of their debts, but the great mass of citizens remained as firmly opposed to him as when they had fought with Wallace. The belief must have hardened in Edward during those unproductive years, in which he had scarcely got beyond the Forth and Clyde, that one man alone stood between him and the unconditional surrender of the country. As long as Wallace lived, intriguing with men such as Lamberton and David of Moravia, the desire for a free and independent Scotland was kept alive in the hearts of the common people, and thus Scotland would never be his.

Edward had no understanding of a people's army. He was accustomed to the feudal warfare of the time. On the capture of one lord, all his vassals at once surrendered, but this was not the case with Wallace. His followers owed their allegiance only to the ideal of freedom that he represented: Balliol's reinstatement, and Scotland for the Scots. Although Wallace's army had been decimated at Falkirk, Edward could foresee, as long as 'that bloody man' remained at large, the certainty of continued opposition to his wishes.

On 9 April 1303 Edward ordered an army of between

10,000 and 12,000 men for a fresh invasion.[1] Bruce was instructed to provide a thousand foot soldiers from Carrick and Galloway, Sir Richard Siward 300 from Nithsdale, and a large contingent from Ireland added to their numbers.

On 16 May 1303 Edward reached Roxburgh and continued on to Edinburgh and Linlithgow. Making a detour to avoid Stirling for the time being, he was in Perth from 11 June to the end of July. He then marched by way of Brechin and Aberdeen to Banff and Elgin, and remained at Kinloss Abbey in Moray from 13 September to 4 October. On 6 November he was back in Dunfermline, where he was joined by the Queen, his second wife, remaining there all winter, until 4 March 1304.

The only opposition he encountered was at Brechin, where Sir Thomas de Maule bravely resisted until killed on the castle wall.

There are two versions of Edward's progress. Hemingburgh reports that the advance was marked by fierce attacks by the English on Scottish-held fortifications; Burton, on the other hand, believes Edward's policy was to placate the Scots;[2] but all that is known about his determination to make the Scots a vassal people tends to refute this. Diplomacy could have achieved as much without an armed invasion.

Wallace is said to have been at either Strathearn or Menteith about this time, and some of his relatives may have urged him to seek the King's peace.[3] Pursuing his unwavering loyalty to an independent Scotland, he refused.

'I say that if all the people of Scotland yield obedience to the King of England, or depart each one from his own freedom, I and my companions who are willing to cleave to me in this matter will stand for the liberty of the Kingdom; and if God aid us we will obey no man save the King or his lieutenant.'[4]

These brave words might well be Wallace's epitaph.

His presence in the area aroused sufficient anxiety in Edward for the King to order the Prince of Wales to send Sir Alexander de Abernethy to keep watch on the River Forth, in case Wallace and his men attempted to cross.

Abernethy apparently wrote to the King, asking what terms should be offered to Wallace should he capitulate. On 3 March 1304 Edward's answer reached him: 'In reply to your request for instructions as to whether it is our pleasure that you should hold out to William le Waleys any words of peace, know that it is not at all our pleasure that you hold out any word of peace to him or to any other of his company, unless they place themselves absolutely and in all things at our will without any reservation whatsoever.'[5]

In other words, only unconditional surrender would be acceptable.

Wallace was certainly under intense pressure at this time. In February Sir John de Segrave, the Warden south of the Forth, was joined by Bruce in an attempt at his capture.[6]

How enthusiastically Bruce pursued this task can only be conjectured. A few months later, in June, he was to begin conspiring with William Lamberton, while outwardly maintaining the appearance of loyalty to Edward. On 11 June Bruce and the Bishop were to sign a secret agreement outlining plans for freeing Scotland from English domination. It was essential for Bruce to have the backing of the Church, and it may well have been that, at Lamberton's persuasion, he got in touch with Wallace. Both conspirators were well aware of the hold Wallace sustained on the affections and loyalty of the people, whose support would be essential in the event of a planned uprising in favour of Bruce. The nobles would once again take sides, but if the Scots rose as one at Wallace's bidding, their intentions had an excellent chance of success.

That Edward was unaware of Bruce's true feelings is evidenced in a letter sent him in March, in which he expressed his pleasure at the diligence with which 'his loyal and faithful Robert de Brus' had lately served him, adding, 'As the robe is well made, you will be pleased to make the hood.'[7]

Earlier that month, Wallace and Sir Simon Fraser had been attacked by Segrave, Sir William de Latimer and Sir Robert de Clifford in Tweeddale and forced to retreat through Lothian.[8] A Scottish turncoat named John of Musselburgh offered to guide the English to Wallace's hideout, and Wallace was brought to bay at Peebles and defeated.[9]

The news was carried to Edward on 12 March, while he was in Aberdeen, and three days later the traitor received 10 shillings from the King's own hand.[10]

Wallace is said to have received prior word of the intended raid from a sympathizer, and it would be interesting to know if the warning came from Bruce.[11]

Although Wallace and Bruce were on opposite sides, it is likely that each was kept informed of the other's activities by Sir Malcolm Wallace, who early on attached himself to Bruce and remained one of his most loyal supporters.

Bruce was generous-hearted enough to acknowledge the debt he owed Wallace, for the latter's example had stirred both himself and Comyn to efforts at throwing off rule by England, which they might well have come to accept once Edward had imposed it determinedly enough on Scotland. In what light, however, he regarded Wallace during the early years of the War of Independence is debatable, and it may have been only in the last year or two of Wallace's life that Bruce came to realize the advantages of winning Wallace over to his side.

Bruce had, after all, little to show for the past eight years. Wallace, on the other hand, had won a great victory at Stirling Bridge, and even Comyn had triumphed at Roslin, whereas all Bruce had achieved were raids in Annandale itself, an attack on Sir William Douglas's lands, and the fiasco of Irvine. He was regarded with a jaundiced eye by many Scots for having participated in the invasions of 1303 and 1304.[12] Lothian was either apathetic or actively hostile to him, and in 1306, when he made his bid for the throne, only a handful of supporters came from the south-east of the country. In Galloway he had found difficulty even in raising his father's vassals,[13] and his popularity in the south was, at best, lukewarm.

If he was to win Scotland, he needed firm support from south of the Forth and Clyde, and only Wallace commanded enough trust and esteem among the populace there to raise a successful uprising in his favour.

How willingly Wallace agreed to back him cannot be stated with any certainty, or even if he allowed himself to be persuaded by his old friend Lamberton.

The years since his return to Scotland must have taken their toll on Wallace. He was a hunted outlaw, constantly under threat of capture or betrayal. Many of his allies had abandoned the struggle and been admitted to Edward's peace. Their efforts to persuade him to do the same having failed must have left him without certain safe houses and supplies of food and arms that previously he had been able to rely upon. Men around him must have tired of living in makeshift shelters and longed for the stability of their own hearths, and finally drifted away as they felt the first frosts of autumn.

In the cruelty of a Scottish winter, the temptation for Wallace to abandon his ideals must have been intense. Yet at no time did he take the soft option by going overseas and quietly disappearing into anonymity. He believed uncompromisingly in freedom for his country. Having determined to resist English domination, he held to his inner faith and never gave up the fight.

Edward was, after all, ageing and in indifferent health. His successor had none of his father's firmness of purpose. The choice on Edward's death of a ruler for Scotland would once again come down to either Bruce or Comyn. Possibly following Wallace's report on his meeting with Balliol, Lamberton must have reached the conclusion that the ex-King's reinstatement was improbable. His attention turned instead to a man strong enough to take and hold Scotland.

Was it now that Lamberton began to influence Wallace into a belief that to back Bruce was the most logical decision for him to take?

If so, Lamberton was already at work on Comyn, for his first step in promoting Bruce was to induce Comyn to abandon his position as Scotland's defender and make peace with Edward. As long as Comyn was identified in the minds of the people as their symbol of resistance, so Bruce would be disregarded. That situation must alter.

On 9 February 1304, after several weeks of negotiation conducted by Lamberton, Comyn and his supporters came to the King's peace at Strathord, in Perthshire.[14] Lamberton also renewed his oath of allegiance and had his lands returned to him.[15] A year earlier, Wishart too had made peace with Edward.[16]

The terms imposed by Edward were particularly easy, possibly not from any benevolence on the King's part but because he was about to besiege Stirling Castle, and all his energies would presently be required for that. Edward thus '... won a spurious reputation for generosity to a land which he had drenched in blood and upon which he had inflicted untold miseries in an unholy attempt to gratify his own selfish ambition'.[17]

Comyn was leniently treated, while the Steward and Sir John de Soulis got away with two years' banishment to their estates south of the River Trent.[18] But Wallace, who still refused to submit, was expressly excluded from the treaty.

'No words of peace are to be held out to William Wallace in any circumstances in our will ... Sir John Comyn, Sir Alexander Lindsay, Sir David Graham and Sir Simon Fraser shall exert themselves until 20 days after Christmas to capture Sir William Wallace and hand him over to the King who will watch to see how each of them conducts himself so that he can do most favour to whoever shall capture Wallace with regard to exile or legal claims or expiation of past misdeeds.'[19]

It is said that Edward had made previous attempts to conciliate Wallace, one by way of Warenne just before the Battle of Stirling Bridge.[20] According to Bower, a royal pardon had been offered, a lordship and lands, even the crown of Scotland held under English suzerainty.[21] To none of these would Wallace yield.

It is well within the bounds of possibility that Edward did make such an offer, his fertile mind perceiving a way of blocking the ambitions of both Bruce and Comyn. With the great lords willing to be persuaded by gifts of one sort or another, such intransigence on the part of Wallace must have fuelled the King's hatred of a man who embodied Scotland's unyielding attitude towards himself. His one, obsessive goal was now to lay hands on him.

Accordingly Edward ordained that James the Steward,

Sir John de Soulis and Sir Ingram de Umfraville were not to be granted letters of safe-conduct until Wallace surrendered.[22] Comyn scorned to associate himself with such shabby manœuvrings and ignored Edward's attempts to use him to capture Wallace, while Sir John de Soulis refused to accept the conditions laid down by Edward, left Scotland and settled in France, where he remained until his death.[23]

During the summer, however, Sir Simon Fraser abandoned Wallace and made peace with Edward.[24] Now the only man whose enmity could give Edward 'a moment's uneasiness' remained defiantly at large and resolutely opposed to all he represented.

As Edward left Dunfermline to direct the siege of Stirling Castle in person, he ordered the magnificent Abbey set on fire, despite its containing the tombs of the Scottish kings and queens, including those of his sister Margaret, her husband, Alexander, and their children.[25] The church and a few cells for the monks were all that remained of an act that demonstrates more clearly than any other the vindictive side of the King.

Two fortified wooden bridges, constructed at King's Lynn to enable Edward's army to cross the River Forth, had been shipped north in parts in thirty vessels and escorted by four warships. The cost amounted to £1,050, a huge sum in those days.[26] Heavy siege-engines were also called up from Edinburgh and Berwick, and orders issued on 1 April to the Earls of Menteith and Strathearn to put a stop to local merchants entering the castle to sell their goods, thus cutting off much-needed supplies of fresh food for the garrison.[27]

By 16 April Sir John Botetourte had joined Bruce in forwarding 'the frame of the great engine of Inverkip'.[28] On 12 April the Prince of Wales had departed for Perth and Dunblane to strip the lead from churches, leaving only that which protected the altars.[29] Such sanctimonious humbug was unlikely to endear Edward to their congregations.

A sidelight on the young prince's activities is gained from his Household Rolls from 20 November 1302 until

November 1303, during most of which time he was in Scotland. He had a lion which he led about on a collar and chain, enjoyed hunting with his hawks and had a setter dog trained to catch partridges. He played dice badly and often lost. He made modest offerings to various saints and more generous gifts of money to his favourites. His stud of horses was particularly fine and cost a considerable sum to maintain, and he was fond of expensive armour and personal apparel.[30]

On 22 April the siege of Stirling Castle began in earnest, backed by at least thirteen engines capable of throwing weights of 100, 200 and 300 pounds.[31] The garrison resisted bravely, an arrow from one of the defenders striking the King's armour as he was directing his troops but failing to pierce it,[32] and a large stone from a mangonel brought down his horse.[33]

Towards the end of June, the English themselves were short of forage and food, but on 20 July the garrison surrendered. It was believed to be 140 strong, but apart from Sir William Oliphant, the constable, who was sent in irons to the Tower, and two friars, it consisted of just twenty-three men.[34]

This hollow victory was concluded in bizarre fashion. An enormous siege-engine called 'the War-Wolf' had not yet come into use.[35] Before evacuation of the castle began, this machine hurled rocks at the fortress to see how effectively it performed, for the entertainment of the Queen and her ladies, who watched from an oriel window in the town.[36]

It is said that Wallace had taken a look at the situation at Stirling but concluded that the English army was too strong to take on. An English force got wind of his whereabouts and pursued him towards Lochearnside but without being able to overtake him.[37] Nevertheless, it demonstrates how unrelenting remained Edward's determination to capture him.

In the same year Edward offered £100 to any man who delivered Wallace to justice.[38]

After a short stay at Holyrood, Edward left on 16 August for the journey home by way of Newcastle, Durham and

York. The Exchequer and other administrative offices were returned to London. It was now only a matter of time, ran the King's thoughts, before the last remaining obstacle to Scotland's total submission was overcome.

15 *Betrayal and Death*

Resolute to live or to die a free man.
Murison

For more than eight years Wallace had held out bravely against Edward. His betrayal, when it occurred, was a murky affair, in which treachery by fellow Scots played a shameful part. On 28 February 1305 a Scots survivor of the siege of Stirling Castle, Ralph de Haliburton, brother of Sir Henry de Haliburton, one of Fraser's Border lieutenants from Kelso, was released from custody in England and handed over to Sir John de Mowbray.[1] Haliburton was to be taken to Scotland '… to help those Scots that were seeking to capture Sir William Wallace'. Haliburton, however, failed in his task.[2]

Edward then offered a bribe in the shape of the heiress of Synton as wife to an Englishman, Edward Keith, afterwards Sheriff of Selkirk, if he would seize Wallace.[3] He too accomplished nothing.

In March 1305 Edward, now an old man by the standards of the time, suffered a seizure, and the hopes of all Scotsmen must have risen with the prospect of a change of monarch. Once again men began to gather round Wallace – about a thousand, with whom he carried out raids all summer.

Well knowing how intensely Edward desired his capture, Wallace could have retreated to France, like de Soulis, and waited for the King's death. Other countries would have been glad to provide him with sanctuary, particularly Norway. Old friends in the Western Isles could have given him shelter and kept him safe from English patrols. Instead, he chose to continue his offensive against the English occupation, knowing that any one of a number of mischances could mean his capture.

Sir John de Menteith, the uncle of Sir John Stewart, who was surrounded and killed at Falkirk, may have nursed a deep resentment that it had been the fault of Wallace. A Scottish knight, he had changed sides and gone over to Edward, being rewarded by being made constable of Dumbartonshire.[4] According to Harry, he was now approached by Sir Aymer de Valence with a view to his capturing Wallace, possibly with the assurance that Wallace's life would be spared. Sir Aymer may also have lent strength to the argument by pointing out that it was Menteith's duty to apprehend the wanted man and that he would earn Edward's highest favour if he complied.

Menteith, at any rate, agreed and is said to have sent his nephew, a boy called Jack Short, to join Wallace's band and report on his movements. There is some suggestion that Wallace may have killed the boy's brother in some dispute or other, and he was thus motivated by a desire for revenge.[5]

Once more, according to Harry, the suspiciously regarded Bruce enters the tale.[6] He was at this time at Edward's Court but, receiving a summons from Wallace to come north and make a bid for the throne, he is supposed to have sent word to Wallace that he would find an excuse to leave England. He promised to meet Wallace on Glasgow Moor on the first night of July.[7]

Wallace, attended by his long-time friend Kerby and Menteith's traitorous nephew, kept the appointment at the house of Robert Rae, one of Menteith's servants, but Bruce did not appear. On succeeding evenings Wallace rode out to Robroyston from Glasgow with the same result. On the eighth night, Menteith, with sixty picked men 'of his own kin and kinsmen born', made his move.

Wallace and Kerby had tired and gone to sleep. Having stealthily disarmed them, Jack Short signalled Menteith that it was safe to approach. It is highly unlikely that Wallace, in expectation of encountering Bruce, would have left neither himself nor the experienced Kerby on guard, and one must suspect the possibility of drugged wine provided by the treacherous Jack Short.

As Menteith burst in upon them, Kerby leapt to his feet and was at once killed. Wallace, finding his weapons gone, bravely defended himself with his bare hands until Menteith came forward and told him resistance was futile. The house was surrounded by English soldiers, but he promised Wallace that his life was in no danger and that he was merely being taken to Dumbarton Castle. Wallace asked him to swear he spoke the truth, and only then allowed his hands to be tied. As they emerged, however, Wallace saw no evidence of English troops and at once knew he had been betrayed.

Whether or not others were involved in Wallace's capture, Sir John Menteith certainly was, and his betrayal has been regarded with detestation by all Scots ever since. A document exists, which appears to be a memoranda of business for Edward's parliament, which denotes 40 marks to be given to the man who spied out Wallace, 60 marks to the others and £100 to Menteith, the arch-traitor.[8]

He continued to enjoy marks of Edward's highest favour. After the middle of September, when Scots commissioners attended the English parliament, in order to agree matters concerning the settlement of their country, nine instead of ten appeared. Earl Patrick was absent, and in his place Menteith '... by the King's command was chosen'.[9] He was confirmed as governor of Dumbarton Castle on 16 June 1306, together with the bishopric of Glasgow. On the same day Edward ordered the chancellor and chamberlain to prepare a charter granting the earldom of Lennox to Menteith.[10]

Some attempt has been made to excuse his actions, but there is no doubt, according to Fordun, de Brunne, the Lanercost chronicler and others, that he was an out-and-out traitor, made worse by the fact that Wallace was said to have been godfather to two of his children.

Now, with all speed and keeping to 'waste land', so as to avoid parts of the country 'where Scotsmen were masters', Menteith ignored Dumbarton Castle and instead made for the Solway Firth.[11] There he handed over his captive to Sir Aymer de Valence and Sir Robert de Clifford, who pressed on with him to Carlisle, where he was imprisoned that night.[12] Sir John de Segrave, the Warden south of the River Forth, now took responsibility for conveying him to London.

From that moment, Wallace was isolated from his friends. His thoughts on the shabbiness of his capture are unknown to us, but that he knew at once that he was a doomed man is certain. He would be aware that he could expect no mercy from Edward, who would shelter behind the travesty of a show trial in order to do him to death. It would, after all, have been easy for Menteith to have killed him at once, had that been the intention. That he had been spared indicated that his end was to be as public and humiliating as possible.

Wallace had always been a very brave young man and, as he rode south to his death, he must have needed to call up all his reserves of courage to face the ordeal that lay ahead of him. Scotland, his beloved country, with its memories, its triumphs and defeats but always with its hold on him, as on all Scots who valued freedom, fell further and further away behind him. He had seen it for the last time.

The hot and tedious journey of seventeen days continued, Wallace riding with his hands roped behind his back and his feet tied beneath his horse's belly.[13] All along the route, the curious came out to watch him go by among his captors.

On Sunday 22 August 1305 the party arrived in London, watched by a large crowd, and Wallace was lodged overnight in the house of Alderman William de Leyre in Fenchurch Street, in the parish of Allhallows Staining.[14] It is not known why he was not taken immediately to the Tower. It is suggested that the mass of people who had turned out to look at the Scottish outlaw might have blocked their route, but it may equally have been that Edward was determined not to honour his opponent with imprisonment in a fortification reserved for the great.

Fiction is full of meetings between historical personages that certainly never occurred but which make dramatically enjoyable reading. One might at first consider one between Edward I and Wallace as falling into this category. Yet, did these two antagonists, in fact, come face to face during Wallace's journey to death?

The *Scalacronica* says, 'He was ... brought before the King of England,' while an anonymous chronicler avers that Wallace was 'presented to the King, but the King would not look at him, and commanded him to London for his trial.'[15]

Was it shame that made Edward look away, because, for all his frequent high moral tone, in the end he had been reduced to the basest of treachery in order to capture him? One may imagine Wallace, well aware that he was going to die, standing straight in front of the King who, despite drenching Scotland in blood for years, had failed to break his country's spirit. One can well accept that Edward must have wanted avidly to see the man who had never bowed the knee to him, in order to satisfy a certain perverse pleasure in the contemplation of his imminent death.

The butchery in store for Wallace makes painful reading.

No time was lost in opening the proceedings against him. Next day, 23 August, he was taken on horseback to Westminster, accompanied by Sir John de Segrave, the mayor, sheriffs and aldermen of London and a huge number of others on horse and on foot.

Arriving at Westminster Hall, Wallace was seated on a bench on the south side, and a wreath of laurel placed on his head.[16] Opinions are divided as to whether this was a sign of mockery or of honour, or to mark an intended victim. Llewelyn's head had been displayed at the Tower crowned with a wreath of ivy, in fulfilment of a prophecy by Merlin.[17] It is difficult to believe that Edward, who had already planned an agonizing and public death for his implacable enemy, would for one moment have considered honouring Wallace.

Is it possible that at some time Wallace was somewhere described, in the ten months he controlled his country's destiny, as the real King of Scotland? He is alleged to have boasted that one day he would be crowned at Westminster, but this is so far from all that is known of his character that the remark can only have stemmed from a malicious tongue.[18] Wallace had steadfastly refused all honours and rewards, accepting only his knighthood. When ruler of Scotland, he had taken no lands to himself, neither estates nor vassals, coronets nor kingly ornament. The only accolade he had ever desired was his country's freedom.

Those appointed on 18 August to try him were Sir John de Seymour, Sir Peter Malory, the lord chief justice, Ralph de Sandwich, the constable of the Tower, John de Bacwell, or Banquelle, a judge, and Sir John le Blound, or Blunt, mayor of London.

Wallace was charged with sedition, homicide, spoliation, robbery, arson and various other felonies. After Balliol's forfeiture of the crown, Edward had publicly received homage from prelates, earls, barons and a multitude of others. He had appointed wardens, lieutenants and sheriffs to maintain his peace and do justice. Yet this Wallace, forgetful of his fealty and allegiance, had risen against his lord; had banded together a great number of felons and feloniously attacked the King's wardens and men; had, in particular, attacked, wounded and slain William de Heselrig, Sheriff of Lanark.

He had assaulted towns, cities and castles of Scotland; had made his writs run throughout the land as if he were Lord Superior of that realm; and, having driven out of Scotland all the wardens and servants of the Lord King, had set up and held parliaments and councils of his own. He had counselled the prelates, earls and barons, his adherents, to submit themselves to the fealty and lordship of the King of France, and to aid that sovereign to destroy the realm of England.[19] He had invaded Northumberland, Cumberland and Westmorland and committed horrible enormities. When Edward had called him to the King's peace, he had rejected his overtures with indignant scorn and refused to submit himself. He had, therefore, been outlawed as 'a misleader of the lieges, a robber, and a felon'.[20]

Wallace, as an outlaw, was not permitted to defend himself on any of the charges and must have realized the hopelessness of trying to do so.[21] Nevertheless, he strenuously denied Sir Peter Malory's assertion that he was a traitor, on the grounds that he had never given Edward his allegiance. On others he doubtless remained silent, contemptuous of the humbug going on around him, as he listened to allegations of putting to death 'old men and young, wives and widows, children and sucklings', of killing priests and nuns and burning down churches, 'together with the bodies of the saints and other relics of them therein placed in honour'.[22]

Of Edward's atrocities at Berwick, his destruction of monasteries, his desecration of St Michael's Church at Linlithgow by turning it into a granary, the burning of Dunfermline Abbey, no mention was made.[23]

Wallace's sentence was then delivered:

> That the said William, for the manifest sedition that he practised against the Lord King himself, by feloniously contriving and acting with a view to his death and to the abasement and submission of his crown and royal dignity, by opposing his liege lord in war to the death, be drawn from the Palace of Westminster to the Tower of London, and from the Tower to Aldgate, and so through the midst of the City, to the Elms;
>
> And that for the robberies, homicides, and felonies he committed in the realm of England and in the land of Scotland, he be there hanged, and afterwards taken down from the gallows;
>
> And that, inasmuch as he was an outlaw, and was not afterwards restored to the peace of the Lord King, he be decollated and decapitated;
>
> And that thereafter, for the measureless turpitude of his deeds towards God and Holy Church in burning down churches ... the heart, the liver, the lungs, and all the internal organs of William's body ... be cast into fire and burned;
>
> And further ... the body of the said Wallace be cut up and divided into four parts; and that the head, so cut off, be set up on London Bridge, in the sight of such as pass by, whether by land or by water; and that one-quarter be hung on a gibbet at Newcastle-upon-Tyne, another quarter at Berwick, a third quarter at Stirling, and the fourth at St Johnson, as a warning and deterrent to all that pass by and behold them.[24]

Wallace was now dragged bound on a hurdle at the tails of horses through a city that had turned out to watch him die. By now, despite his strong young frame, he was undoubtedly spent and close to exhaustion, for there are a hundred ways in which captors may torment a prisoner in their charge. He had been roughed up at the time of his capture by Menteith's men, had ridden roped to a horse for almost three weeks, and had been inadequately fed and locked overnight in the most noisome of cells, for there was no point in according a doomed man privileges. Now he was exposed in humiliating fashion to the gaze of a citizenry eager to share the excitement of his butchery.

The place of execution was at the Elms in Smithfield, later Cow Lane and then renamed King Street. At the foot of the gallows, Wallace is said to have requested a priest to hear his confession. Harry has the Archbishop of Canterbury defying Edward and giving Wallace absolution, but it is unlikely he would have dared arouse the King's fury in such a way.[25]

Some other priest came forward, for Harry records that Wallace asked Clifford to let him have the psalter he always carried. When this was done, Wallace requested the priest to hold it open before him '… till they to him had done all that they would'.[26]

Matthew of Westminster, the English chronicler, gloats over Wallace's sufferings: 'He was hung in a noose, and afterwards let down half-living; next his genitals were cut off and his bowels torn out and burned in a fire; then and not till then his head was cut off and his trunk cut into four pieces.'[27]

As the crowds drifted away, their entertainment over, Wallace's head was placed on a spike and carried to London Bridge. Before long, it was to be joined by those of other distinguished victims, his brother John, the Earl of Atholl and Sir Simon Fraser.

His right leg was taken to Berwick, the left to Perth, his left arm to Stirling, and his right arm hung above the bridge at Newcastle-upon-Tyne 'over the common sewer'.

Sir John de Segrave received 10 shillings for conveying Wallace's dismembered body, in accordance with Edward's wishes, 'for terror and rebuke to all who should pass by and behold them'.[28]

There is a local tradition that, when the flesh had fallen away, monks from Cambuskenneth Abbey went at dead of night to collect what remained of the left arm. This they buried in the abbey grounds, the hand outstretched and pointing towards Abbey Craig, the site of Wallace's superb victory, where today stands the magnificent monument to the memory of a great patriot.

16   *The Man of Destiny*

The study of all history ... convinces us that no single man
... can in the end prevail over a whole people.

Bain

Edward doubtless slept soundly on the night of 23 August
1305, well pleased with the day's events. Resistance to his
rule in Scotland had finally been ended. Comyn and Bruce
were his. Wallace was dead. There would be no further
trouble north of the Border.

This was however, far from the truth, and once again
Edward had misjudged the spirit of the Scots. They heard
of Wallace's death with a deepening hatred for the King
who had consigned him to a barbaric execution. Great
lords had been forgiven their treachery time and again,
whereas the one man who had never sworn allegiance to
England had been mercilessly put to death.

Did Edward demand an eyewitness account of the
cruelties inflicted on Wallace? From what has been
gathered of his nature, one can be confident that he
wanted to know every detail of his enemy's dying.

> The death of Wallace stands forth among the violent ends
> which have a memorable place in history [writes Burton].
> Proverbially such acts belong to a policy that outwits itself.
> But the retribution has seldom come so quickly, and so
> utterly in defiance of all human preparation and
> calculation, as here. Of the bloody trophies sent to frighten
> a broken people into abject subjection, the bones had not
> yet been bared ere they became tokens to deepen the
> wrath and strengthen the courage of a people arising to try
> the strength of the bonds by which they were bound and,
> if possible, break them once and for all.[1]

Bruce has been accused of being a witness at both the trial and execution of Wallace, principally because at the time he stood high in Edward's favour.[2] Although Bruce was in London for the Lent Parliament of 28 February to 21 March, he was not present at the parliament summoned by the King in September, three weeks after Wallace's death, when ten Scottish commissioners were named as the new governors of Scotland.[3]

The accusation bears some consideration, hinging as it does on the relationship between Bruce and Wallace. Both men, in their separate ways, fought for their country's freedom, but Wallace's was ever the nobler aim. He desired nothing for himself, neither crown nor possessions, endured much and never, despite the offer of bribes and inducements, relinquished his stand against tyranny.

Bruce, by contrast, held to his determination to shake off English rule because he believed himself entitled to be his country's king. This entailed active opposition to Wallace as the representative of Balliol's reinstatement, particularly after 1302, when he sided once again with Edward. Bruce is, however, innocent of the charge of attending Wallace's execution, for he had returned to Scotland after 21 March.[4]

Some time between the summer and autumn of 1305 Edward's attitude towards Bruce underwent a dramatic change. In a conspicuous slight, he was omitted from the list of those appointed to administer Scottish affairs, whereas Lamberton, Bishop of St Andrews, who had been Wallace's friend and ally for so long, was named one of the commissioners.[5] In addition, those lands of Sir Ingram de Umfraville which had been given to Bruce a few months before were taken from him and returned to their owner.[6]

He was ordered, in addition, to give up Kildrummy Castle, an important fortification in Moray, on 15 September 1305.[7]

On 26 October four temporary guardians of Scotland were named, but Bruce was not among them. Nor was he included among the twenty-one sheriffs also appointed, although he had until lately been sheriff of Lanark and constable of Ayr Castle.

So far out of favour was Bruce that during 1305 and 1306

Edward even demanded the repayment of debts owed by his father twenty years earlier.

It has been suggested that Wallace's death was the reason for Bruce's breaking with Edward, and Bruce's expression of his disgust at the barbarity of Wallace's end may well have reached Edward's ears.[8] But it is obvious that it was the King who now distanced himself from a man he had begun to distrust. If the documents found on Wallace implicated Bruce, we have the answer.[9]

That the King's advisers used spies has already become apparent from reports that have come down to us. The quarrel between Comyn and Bruce after Falkirk is one instance. How fully Edward trusted Bruce after 1302 is debatable. Several times the King placed him in situations in which he was obliged to demonstrate his loyalty by opposing Scotland: raising troops or fetching siege-engines to be used against the nationalist army.

It needed only a whisper to suggest that Bruce was conspiring with others to alter Edward's confidence in him, and this may well have occurred after Wallace's death. Jealousies and intrigue existed in any Court, where men strove to please a monarch who could generously reward them, and Bruce could well have been the focus of these. He had, after all, unlike other lords who had remained faithful to Edward, changed sides more than once, and might do so again.

It must have seemed to Bruce, following Wallace's end, that the time had come for him to act decisively in his own interests.

Accordingly, he approached Comyn with a proposition.[10] One of them should support the other for the crown of Scotland, with the loser receiving the winner's estates and possessions. Comyn agreed, and documents were signed and exchanged to that effect.

That Comyn had no intention of keeping to the agreement is evident by his sending word of it to Edward.[11] It has been suggested that he either lost his nerve or hoped to be rewarded by the King, but it may equally well have been that he saw an opportunity of ridding himself once and for all of his deadliest rival.[12]

No matter they had signed a mutually advantageous agreement, Comyn and Bruce were on opposing sides and always had been. Comyn would remember how Bruce and his father had refused to surrender Carlisle Castle to the nationalist army in 1296; that he had never acknowledged his kinsman, Balliol, as king; how he had made his peace with Edward when he himself was holding on as representative of his country's resistance. Long-festering resentments were undoubtedly at work which were to have fatal consequences for himself.

In January 1306 Bruce returned to the English Court, by which time Edward strongly suspected him for a traitor. While dining with friends, the King remarked, perhaps with a cold smile, that he planned to arrest Bruce and try him for treason.[13]

That information was passed to Bruce by a friend, and he at once took horse for Scotland. It is likely the King added that he was awaiting proof (Edward's legal mind would demand more than the word of a Comyn), which Bruce would interpret as the signed agreement's being on its way to England, for he met Comyn's messenger riding towards London, searched the man, discovered the document and killed him.[14]

There was now no turning back.

At his castle of Dalswinton, near Dumfries, Comyn received a message inviting him to meet Bruce on 10 February at the church of the Friars Minor in Dumfries.[15] Undoubtedly the choice of venue was designed to reassure Comyn that Bruce knew nothing of his treachery and that he could count on being safe in sanctified surroundings. However, the moment they met, each man accused the other of betrayal. Bruce drew his dagger and stabbed Comyn. His uncle, Sir Robert Comyn, struck with his own weapon at Bruce, but the blade was deflected by his armour, and he was cut down by Christopher Seton, husband of Bruce's sister Christina.[16]

As both men fled, they encountered Robert Kirkpatrick, another of Bruce's party, in the doorway of the church. On his demanding to know what had happened, Bruce answered, 'I doubt that I have slain "Red" Comyn.'

'Do you doubt? Then I'll make sure,' answered Kirkpatrick, who entered the church and delivered Comyn a death blow.[17]

It has always been a matter of conjecture whether the murder of Comyn was planned as part of a *coup d'état* or was a totally unpremeditated act.[18] Once Bruce realized he had been betrayed to Edward, he had the choice of being arrested for treason or disposing of Comyn and making a bid for the crown. All, therefore, points to his meeting Comyn with the intention of forcing the issue by the only solution that made sense to him.

The speed with which he now rode to the Bishop of Glasgow, to make confession and receive absolution, suggests that Wishart had been well prepared for some such decisive action on the part of Bruce and saw it as the signal for an uprising that would give Bruce the throne.[19]

On the face of it, to have committed murder in a holy building was an act of utter folly and should have meant immediate excommunication by the Church. The question never arose, for the Scottish clergy rallied at once to the support of the man who had sworn in secret agreement with Lamberton the previous year to defend its liberty. Six months later, on Palm Sunday, 27 March 1306, Bruce was crowned King Robert I in the Chapel Royal of Scone, claiming the throne by virtue of his Celtic blood.[20]

The importance of that claim is shown by the fact that ten of the fifteen companions at his coronation came from the old Celtic kingdom north of the Forth and Clyde and were of considerably greater standing than the five from the south.[21] Support for Bruce, even six months after he had been crowned, remained indifferent or even hostile to him south of the Antonine Line.[22]

The Bishops of Glasgow, St Andrews and Moray, the three most powerful churchmen in Scotland, with the Abbot of Scone, officiated at the ceremony.

It would be pleasing to round off the story of Scotland's struggle for independence by relating that Edward accepted the new régime and that peace followed. The facts were, however, very different. The fortunes of Bruce were to ebb and flow, at times reaching a nadir of disaster, before he bravely gathered himself once again to continue the fight.

In 1306 his army was defeated at Methven, and although he himself escaped, his brother Nigel was captured at Kildrummy Castle and executed. His brother-in-law the Earl of Atholl was likewise captured and executed in 1306. The same fate came to his brothers Alexander and Thomas a year later, and in 1307 Sir John Wallace, William Wallace's brother, was executed in London. Sir Simon Fraser, who had fought with Wallace, was also taken at Kildrummy and met his death in London, his head being fixed on a spike next to Wallace's on London Bridge.

The Bishop of Glasgow was captured at Cupar in Fife early in June 1306 and, with the Bishop of St Andrews and the Abbot of Scone, went as prisoner to England, Wishart to Porchester, Lamberton to Winchester Castle.[23] Wishart was not to be released until nine years later, a frail and almost blind old man, dying two years later. Lamberton, however, was astute enough to make his peace with Edward and remained sufficiently in favour to serve his son, Edward II.[24]

As soon as Bruce made his bid for the throne, the north rose in his support. The whole of the northern clergy and seventy-eight leading citizens came out for him in defiance of Edward. The Earls of Atholl, Menteith and Strathearn were among sixteen from Perthshire, and there were twelve from Angus, twelve from Fife, eleven from Aberdeen and Banff, eleven from Moray, six from Lennox, four from Stirling, four from Argyll and one each from Dumbarton and Clackmannan who declared for Bruce.[25] Among those from Moray were Sir William de Moray of Sandford, Sir Alan de Moray of Culbin and Sir Walter de Moray, all kinsmen of the late Andrew de Moray. David de Moravia's support of Bruce particularly infuriated Edward. The King was reported as having 'the ill-will of the said Bishop very much at heart'.[26]

Although threatened with excommunication by the Pope, the Scottish Church never wavered from its support of Bruce.[27]

In the summer of 1308 Bruce tackled the Comyn

problem, with a view to a final solution. For the past two years he had been strongly opposed by the Comyns, for they were fighting not against Scotland but against the murderer of their kinsman. Bruce launched an attack which captured their castles, destroyed their lands, subdued their vassals and drove them headlong from Aberdeenshire following the Battle of Inverurie.[28] The Comyns under the Earl of Buchan retreated from Fyfie, pursued by Edward Bruce, brother of the King, and were utterly destroyed at Old Deer.[29]

By then, Edward I was dead. He had received – with disbelief and rage – the news of Comyn's death and Bruce's rebellion when at Winchester.[30] Although he was far from well, he at once set about planning an invasion of Scotland.

Reaching Cumberland in the summer of 1307, he fell so ill that he was unable to continue his march. His mind began to wander, and he swore a curious oath 'before God and the swans' to overwhelm Scotland once and for all.[31] After he had accomplished that, he would fight no more but return to the Holy Land and end his days there.

Realizing he was dying, he gave orders that his heart was to be sent to Palestine and the flesh boiled from his body, while his bones were to be wrapped in a bull's hide and carried at the head of his army. He died facing the Solway at Burgh-on-Sands on 7 July 1307.

His son ignored his father's bizarre instructions and sent his corpse, bones and all, to Waltham Abbey to await a royal burial.[32]

The new King, Edward II, was to be murdered by his guards at Berkeley Castle, Gloucestershire, in 1327, after having been forced by his barons to abdicate in favour of his son.

Edward I's death proved to be a turning-point in the fortunes of Scottish resistance. It would, however, take the decisive Battle of Bannockburn, on 24 June 1314, for Bruce finally to win his country's independence.

Employing the same tactics as Wallace at Stirling Bridge and Falkirk, he deployed his troops in schiltrons behind the water-logged meadows that fringed the Bannock Burn, in which the English heavy cavalry floundered hopelessly and archers could not find firm footholds to manœuvre.[33]

Among those unhorsed who took refuge in under-growth after the battle was Sir Marmaduke de Twenge. Next day he emerged in his shirt-sleeves, found Bruce and knelt before him. Bruce, who probably knew him well, said mildly, 'Welcome, Sir Marmaduke. To what man art thou prisoner?', to which the reply was, 'To none would I yield but you.' Bruce then drew the knight to his feet, took him to his royal tent to recover and treated him kindly.[34]

The disaster for the English at Bannockburn was so overwhelming that it was taken at the time as a special punishment by Heaven for the nation's wrongdoing.[35]

The victory of Bannockburn won Scotland her freedom, but it should never be forgotten what was owed to those who had sacrificed much, and in some cases all, to keep the flame of resistance bright. Of these, the name of William Wallace, a generous and chivalric foe, according even to English chroniclers, a man of vision, courage and nobility of spirit, must ever stand high in the memory and esteem of all for whom freedom is not merely a word but a dearly won way of life.

Bibliography

Andrews, Allen, *Kings and Queens of England and Scotland* (Marshall Cavendish, 1986)

Bain, J., *The Edwards in Scotland* (Edinburgh, 1901)

Barron, Evan Macleod, *The Scottish War of Independence* (Robert Carruthers & Sons, Inverness, 1934)

Barrow, G.W.S., *Kingship and Unity: Scotland 1000-1306* (Edward Arnold, 1981)

Bingham, Caroline, *The Crowned Lions* (David & Charles, 1978)

Brown, P. Hume, *History of Scotland*, Vol. 1 (Cambridge University Press, 1911)

Buchan, John, *The Massacre of Glencoe* (Buchan & Enright, 1985)

Carruth, J.A., *Heroic Wallace and Bruce* (Jarrold & Sons, 1986)

Delderfield, E.R., *Kings & Queens of England and Great Britain* (David & Charles, 1970)

Fergusson, James, *William Wallace, Guardian of Scotland* (Alexander Maclehose & Co, 1938)

Fisher, Andrew, *William Wallace* (John Donald, Edinburgh, 1986)

Kermack, W.R., *The Scottish Highlands* (W. & A.K. Johnston & G.W. Bacon, 2nd edn., 1967)

Kightly, Charles, *Folk Heroes of Britain* (Thames & Hudson, 1982)

MacLean, Fitzroy, *A Concise History of Scotland* (Thames & Hudson, 1970)

Maurois, André, *A History of England* (Bodley Head, 3rd edn., 1968)

Murison, A.F., *Sir William Wallace* (Famous Scots Series, Oliphant, Anderson & Ferrier, Edinburgh, 1898)

New Encyclopaedia Britannica, 15th edn. (William Benton, 1974)

Newton, Toyne, *The Demonic Connection* (Blandford, 1987)

Platt, Colin, *The English Medieval Town* (Secker & Warburg, 1976)

Powicke, Sir Maurice, *The Thirteenth Century, 1216–1307* (Clarendon, Oxford, 1962)

Salzman, L.F., *Edward I* (Constable, 1968)

Scott, Ronald McNair, *Robert the Bruce* (Hutchinson, 1982)

Stones, E.L.G., ed. and trans. *Anglo-Scottish Relations 1174–1328* (Oxford, 1970)

Thorne, J.O. and Collocott, T.C., *Chambers Biographical Dictionary* (Chambers, 1974)

Tomkeieff, O.G., *Life in Norman England* (Batsford, 2nd edn., 1967)

References

Chapter 1
1   Maurois, p.152
2   Barron, p.216
3   Barron, p.212
4   Barron, p.189
5   Barron, p.387
6   Barron, p.211
7   Barron, p.327
8   Kermack, p.32
9   Barron, p.218
10 Brown, p.58
11 Barron, p.216
12 Barron, p.217
13 Barron, p.216
14 Powicke, p.581
15 Powicke, p.581
16 Kermack, p.42
17 Kermack, p.42
18 Barron, p.189
19 Brown, p.77
20 Brown, p.80
21 Brown, p.83
22 Powicke, p.586
23 Barrow, p.113
24 Powicke, p.571
25 Brown, p.96
26 Brown, p.98
27 Powicke, p.592
28 Powicke, p.596
29 Murison, p.29

Chapter 2
1   Powicke, p.572
2   Barron, p.187
3   Brown, p.18
4   Buchan, p.35
5   Barron, p.189
6   Scott, p.4

7   Scott, p.5
8   Powicke, p.573
9   Brown, p.105
10 Brown, p.14
11 Powicke, p.573
12 Barron, p.14
13 Barron, p.64
14 Barron, p.14
15 Fergusson, p.35
16 Powicke, p.575
17 Scott, p.5
18 Tomkeieff, p.18
19 Platt, p.47
20 Tomkeieff, p.77
21 Platt, p.37
22 Bingham, p.183
23 Platt, p.99
24 Barron, p.26
25 Barron, p.27
26 Powicke, p.670
27 Powicke, p.678
28 Barron, p.439
29 Bingham, p.182
30 Powicke, p.549
31 Barron, p.437
32 Powicke, p.549
33 Salzman, p.185
34 Salzman, p.184
35 Tomkeiff, p.21
36 Salzman, p.183
37 Barron, p.439

Chapter 3
1   Bain, p.5
2   Murison, p.44
3   Murison, p.43
4   Murison, p.44
5   Fergusson, p.6

6   Carruth, p.5
7   Fergusson, p.5
8   Fergusson, p.5
9   Murison, p.42
10 Brown, p.41
11 Fergusson, p.6
12 Murison, p.42
13 Murison, p.45
14 Murison, p.46
15 Murison, p.59
16 Murison, p.48
17 Fergusson, p.7
18 Fergusson, p.8
19 Barron, p.213
20 Murison, p.48
21 Murison, p.49
22 Murison, p.44
23 Kightly, p.153
24 Chambers, p.636
25 Chambers, p.636
26 Barron, p. 156
27 Murison, p.48
28 Murison, p.49
29 Murison, p.50
30 Murison, p.50
31 Murison, p.50
32 Murison, p.50
33 Murison, p.52
34 Murison, p.52
35 Murison, p.54
36 Murison, p.54

Chapter 4
1   Salzman, p.134
2   Salzman, p.182
3   Salzman, p.182
4   Salzman, p.127
5   Bain, p.34
6   Bain, p.34
7   Salzman, p.127
8   Barron, p.98
9   Powicke, p.229
10 Newton, p.53
11 Newton, p.53
12 Newton, p.53
13 Newton, p.54
14 Newton, p.54
15 Bingham, p.153
16 Bingham, p.153
17 Maurois, p.152

18 Scott, p.14
19 Tomkeieff, p.123
20 Murison, p.102
21 Andrews, p.52
22 Andrews, p.52
23 Delderfield, p.50
24 Salzman, p.213
25 Powicke, p.672
26 Murison, p.130
27 Bain, p.34
28 Fergusson, p.216
29 Brown, p.126
30 Barron, p.90

Chapter 5
1   Brown, p.102
2   Brown, p.103
3   Brown, p.103
4   Murison, p.11
5   Bain, p.22
6   Murison, p.13
7   Powicke, p.587
8   Scott, p.11
9   Powicke, p.587
10 Scott, p.10
11 Scott, p.11
12 Scott, p.11
13 Scott, p.19
14 Murison, p.13
15 Scott, p.19
16 Murison, p.15
17 Murison, p.15
18 Murison, p.15
19 Murison, p.17
20 Murison, p.17
21 Scott, p.20
22 Murison, p.17
23 Murison, p. 17
24 Scott, p.21
25 Fergusson, p.9
26 Maurois, p.151
27 Brown, p.109
28 Murison, p.18
29 MacLean, p.35
30 Bain, p.22
31 Bain, p.23
32 Murison, p.21
33 Brown, p.110
34 Brown, p.110
35 Brown, p.110

36 Brown, p.110
37 Murison, p.23
38 Murison, p.23
39 Powicke, p.606
40 *Encyclopaedia Britannica*, p.84
41 Powicke, p.607
42 Stones, p.117
43 Scott, p.33
44 Barron, p.114
45 Scott, p.33
46 Brown, p.113
47 Powicke, p.608
48 Powicke, p.610
49 Powicke, p.612
50 Brown, p.113
51 *Chambers*, p.442
52 Brown, p.114
53 Scott, p.34
54 Brown, p.114
55 Brown, p.115
56 Scott, p.34

Chapter 6
1 Murison, p.52
2 Murison, p.57
3 Murison, p.57
4 Murison, p.57
5 Murison, p.57
6 Murison, p.57
7 Murison, p.58
8 *Chambers*, p.1320
9 Murison, p.58
10 Murison, p.58
11 Murison, p.59
12 Murison, p.59
13 Murison, p.59
14 Murison, p.59
15 Murison, p.60
16 Murison, p.60
17 Murison, p.60
18 Murison, p.61
19 Fergusson, p.34
20 Scott, p.34
21 Scott, p.34
22 Fergusson, p.11
23 Murison, p.34
24 Salzman, p.121
25 Salzman, p.121
26 Salzman, p.121
27 Fergusson, p.12

28 Salzman, p.122
29 Scott, p.35
30 Scott, p.35
31 Fergusson, p.12
32 Powicke, p.614
33 Murison, p.35
34 Scott, p.36
35 Fergusson, p.14
36 Fergusson, p.14
37 Powicke, p.614
38 Scott, p.36
39 Powicke, p.614
40 Barron, p.116
41 Scott, p.241
42 Powicke, p.615
43 Salzman, p.148
44 Powicke, p.615
45 Murison, p.38
46 Brown, p.117
47 Powicke, p.614
48 Bain, p.27
49 Brown, p.117
50 Salzman, p.125
51 Fergusson, p.40
52 Salzman, p.139
53 Fergusson, p.16
54 Powicke, p.618
55 Fergusson, p.3

Chapter 7
1 Powicke, p.585
2 Murison, p.50
3 Scott, p.40
4 Barron, p.76
5 Barron, p.79
6 Barron, p.76
7 Barron, p.205
8 Barron, p.76
9 Barron, p.205
10 Barron, p.79
11 Barron, p.201
12 Barron, p.206
13 Barron, p.207
14 Barron, p.79
15 Scott, p.38
16 Murison, p.61
17 Murison, p.61
18 Murison, p.61
19 Murison, p.62
20 Murison, p.63

21 Murison, p.63
22 Carruth, p.5
23 Murison, p.63
24 Murison, p.66
25 Maurois, p.248
26 Murison, p.66
27 Murison, p.66
28 Murison, p.66
29 Murison, p.67
30 Murison, p.68
31 Murison, p.69
32 Fergusson, p.120
33 Murison, p.69
34 Murison, p.70
35 Murison, p.69
36 Murison, p.69
37 Murison, p.69
38 Murison, p.69
39 Murison, p.60
40 Murison, p.70
41 Murison, p.71
42 Murison, p.57
43 Murison, p.52
44 Fergusson, p.21
45 Murison, p.53
46 Murison, p.53
47 Murison, p.53
48 Murison, p.72
49 Murison, p.53
50 Murison, p.73
51 Murison, p.53
52 Murison, p.51
53 Murison, p.73

Chapter 8
 1 Fergusson, p.22
 2 Murison, p.73
 3 Murison, p.73
 4 Barron, p.24
 5 Barron, p.24
 6 Barron, p.28
 7 Murison, p.74
 8 Murison, p.74
 9 Murison, p.75
10 Murison, p.75
11 Barron, p.43
12 Barron, p.44
13 Barron, p.44
14 Barron, p.26
15 Scott, p.39

16 Murison, p.77
17 p.11
18 Murison, p.76
19 Fergusson, p.25
20 Murison, p.76
21 Fergusson, p.25
22 Barron, p.22
23 Barron, p.27
24 Murison, p.76
25 Murison, p.76
26 Powicke, p.580
27 Murison, p.83
28 Barron, p.42
29 Scott, p.44
30 Barron, p.21
31 Murison, p.83
32 Barron, p.78
33 Murison, p.83
34 Barron, p.60
35 Barron, p.60
36 Murison, p.85
37 Murison, p.79
38 Fergusson, p.28
39 Murison, p.78
40 Murison, p.79
41 Murison, p.78
42 Murison, p.79
43 Murison, p.79
44 Murison, p.79
45 Murison, p.79
46 Barron, p.120
47 Murison, p.80
48 Barron, p.30
49 Fergusson, p.33

Chapter 9
 1 Murison, p.80
 2 Fergusson, p.36
 3 Murison, p.81
 4 Murison, p.84
 5 Murison, p.84
 6 Murison, p.84
 7 Murison, p.84
 8 Murison, p.84
 9 Barron, p.60
10 Murison, p.85
11 Barron, p.60
12 Fergusson, p.38
13 Barron, p.62
14 Barron, p.62

15 Murison, p.85
16 Fergusson, p.44
17 Murison, p.85
18 Barron, p.68
19 Murison, p.85
20 Barron, pp.74–84
21 Murison, p.85
22 Murison, p.85
23 Murison, p.85
24 Murison, p.85
25 Fergusson, p.57
26 Murison, p.86
27 Murison, p.85
28 Fergusson, p.49
29 Murison, p.87
30 Salzman, p. 140
31 Murison, p.86
32 Murison, p.86
33 Fergusson, p.60
34 Murison, p.87
35 Fergusson, p.67
36 Murison, p.87
37 Murison, p.87
38 Fergusson, p.60
39 Fergusson, p.66
40 Murison, p.87
41 Fergusson, p.75
42 Powicke, p.687
43 Barron, p.33
44 Barron, p.72
45 Barron, p.205
46 Barron, p.205

Chapter 10
 1 Fergusson, p.74
 2 Murison, p.87
 3 Fergusson, p.75
 4 Barron, p.70
 5 Murison, p.90
 6 Fergusson, p.73
 7 Murison, p.93
 8 Fergusson, p.95
 9 Murison, p.99
10 Scott, p.47
11 Fergusson, p.99
12 Fergusson, p.104
13 Scott, p.47
14 Scott, p.48
15 Fergusson, p.73
16 Murison, p.93

17 Murison, p.93
18 Fergusson, p.91
19 Murison, p.93
20 Murison, p.94
21 Fergusson, p.85
22 Murison, p.94
23 Murison, p.94
24 Murison, p.94
25 Murison, p.94
26 Fergusson, p.89
27 Murison, p.95
28 Murison, p.96
29 Fergusson, p.89
30 Fergusson, p.89
31 Murison, p.97
32 Fergusson, p.108
33 Fergusson, p.110
34 Murison, p.92
35 Murison, p.92
36 Murison, p. 91
37 Fergusson, p.104
38 Fergusson, p.104
39 Fergusson, p.105
40 Murison, p.99
41 Fergusson, p.108

Chapter 11
 1 Murison, p.98
 2 Murison, p.98
 3 Murison, p.98
 4 Powicke, p.688
 5 Murison, p.100
 6 Powicke, p.689
 7 Fergusson, p.116
 8 Murison, p.100
 9 Murison, p.100
10 Fergusson, p.117
11 Fergusson, p.128
12 Fergusson, p.128
13 Fergusson, p.128
14 Murison, p.100
15 Maurois, p.151
16 Murison, p.100
17 Murison, p.100
18 Fergusson, p.131
19 Fergusson, p.132
20 Murison, p.102
21 Murison, p.102
22 Fergusson, p.135
23 Barron, p.77

24 Fergusson, p.142
25 Brown, p.119
26 Barron, p.77
27 Barron, p.78
28 Murison, p.103
29 Murison, p.103
30 Murison, p.154
31 Brown, p.119
32 Fergusson, p.119
33 Fergusson, p.121
34 Murison, p.103
35 Fergusson, p.123
36 Murison, p. 103
37 Murison, p. 105
38 Murison, p. 106
39 Fergusson, p.157
40 Fergusson, p.151
41 Fergusson, p.151
42 Murison, p.108

Chapter 12
1   Murison, p.108
2   Murison, p.108
3   Barron, p.117
4   Murison, p.108
5   Barron, p.125
6   Powicke, p.692
7   Fergusson, p.157
8   Fergusson, p.157
9   Murison, p.109
10 Bain, p.30
11 Murison, p.118
12 Murison, p.119
13 Powicke, p.696
14 Fergusson, p.165
15 Barron, p.130
16 Fergusson, p.167
17 Murison, p.118
18 Murison, p.120
19 Murison, p.121
20 Murison, p.120
21 Powicke, p.696
22 Barron, p.130
23 Fergusson, p.170
24 Fergusson, p.174
25 Barron, p.130
26 Murison, p.121
27 Powicke, p.696
28 Murison, p.122
29 Scott, p.56

30 Murison, p.123
31 Murison, p.123
32 Bain, p.32
33 Bain, p.32
34 Murison, p.124
35 Murison, p.124
36 Powicke, p.694
37 Barron, p.144
38 Bain, p.33
39 Barron, p.142
40 Murison, p.125
41 Murison, p.126
42 Powicke, p.710
43 Powicke, p.710
44 Brown, p.44

Chapter 13
1   Murison, p.111
2   Murison, p.112
3   Murison, p.112
4   Murison, p.112
5   Murison, p.113
6   Murison, p.114
7   Murison, p.114
8   Murison, p.114
9   Murison, p.113
10 Fergusson, p.175
11 Murison, p.133
12 Powicke, p.694
13 Scott, p.61
14 Murison, p.127
15 Barron, p.102
16 Barron, p.108
17 Barron, p.298
18 Barron, p.144
19 Bain, p.40
20 Murison, p.128
21 Murison, p.128
22 Barron, p.86

Chapter 14
1   Bain, p.40
2   Murison, p.129
3   Bain, p.42
4   Fergusson, p.186
5   Fergusson, p.189
6   Powicke, p.709
7   Murison, p.137
8   Fergusson, p.190

9   Murison, p.139
10 Fergusson, p.190
11 Scott, p.69
12 Barron, p.140
13 p. 109
14 Powicke, p.709
15 Powicke, p.710
16 Murison, p.137
17 Barron, p.154
18 Murison, p.135
19 Fergusson, p.191
20 Murison, p.135
21 Murison, p.136
22 Murison, p.140
23 Fergusson, p.192
24 Murison, p.134
25 Murison, p.130
26 Bain, p.40
27 Murison, p.130
28 Murison, p.131
29 Murison, p.131
30 Bain, p.44
31 Murison, p.131
32 Murison, p.131
33 Scott, p.70
34 Murison, p.132
35 Murison, p.131
36 Murison, p.131
37 Murison, p.140
38 Salzman, p.163

Chapter 15
1   Bain, p.45
2   Murison, p.140
3   Bain, p.45
4   Murison, p.142
5   Murison, p.142
6   Murison, p.142
7   Murison, p.142
8   Murison, p.144
9   Murison, p.144
10 Murison, p.144
11 Murison, p.142
12 Murison, p.143
13 Fergusson, p.211
14 Fergusson, p.212
15 Fergusson, p.211
16 Fergusson, p.213

17 Murison, p.145
18 Murison, p.145
19 Murison, p.146
20 Murison, p.147
21 Murison, p.147
22 Murison, p.147
23 Fergusson, p.216
24 Murison, p.147
25 Murison, p.148
26 Murison, p.148
27 Fergusson, p.217
28 Fergusson, p.217

Chapter 16
1   Murison, p.150
2   Barron, p.159
3   Barron, p.163
4   Barron, p.162
5   Barron, p.165
6   Barron, p.165
7   Scott, p.71
8   Barron, p.172
9   Barron, p.172
10 Scott, p.71
11 Powicke, p.713
12 Scott, p.72
13 Scott, p.72
14 Scott, p.73
15 Powicke, p.713
16 Scott, p.73
17 Scott, p.73
18 Brown, p.211
19 Scott, p.74
20 Barron, p.213
21 Barron, p.214
22 Barron, p.277
23 Barron, p.243
24 Bain, p.50
25 Barron, p.227
26 Barron, p.240
27 Barron, p.378
29 Barron, p.328
30 Bain, p.48
31 Maurois, p.152
32 Scott, p.104
33 Brown, p.129
34 Scott, p.163
35 Brown, p.130

Index